# WHO ARE YOU, GOD?
## . . . and What Are You Like?

---

# A Student Discussion Manual on the Attributes of God

---

**Dawson McAllister**
**and**
**Rich Miller**

# Who Are You, God?

## AND WHAT ARE YOU LIKE?

A Student Discussion Manual on the
Attributes of God

## Dawson McAllister and Rich Miller

SHEPHERD MINISTRIES

# DAWSON McALLISTER

Dawson is one of America's outstanding youth communicators. He has been a youth pastor, coffee house counsellor, author, TV host and friend to thousands of teenagers.

After academic study at Bethel College in Minnesota and Talbot Theological Seminary in California, Dawson became involved in a program for runaways and desperate teenagers that has developed into a nation-wide ministry. His practical experience and spiritual insight make him much-in-demand as a speaker at assemblies, weekend seminars, conferences and camps.

A series of prime time TV specials entitled "Kids in Crisis" has enabled him to provide spiritual counsel to teenage youth throughout the nation. Nine popular discussion manuals, five video programs and a film series have multiplied his ministry to individuals and small groups.

With a heart full of compassion for kids and gifted with a magnetic personality, Dawson is committed to seeing that today's youth have a chance to hear the facts about how Jesus Christ changes lives.

Dawson lives with his wife and two sons on a historic farm outside of Nashville, Tennessee where he enjoys breaking and training horses in his spare time.

# RICH MILLER

Rich is a vibrant, athletic youth leader who has been associated with Campus Crusade for 13 years working with high school students. He originally planned to be a weather forecaster and took his BS degree from Penn State in meterology.

One outstanding experience in Rich's career was the year he spent traveling with Josh McDowell. In 1980 he went to California and earned a Masters degree in Christian apologetics at the Simon Greenleaf School of Law in Anaheim. He also has written for Campus Life magazine.

Rich Miller lives in Warminster, outside of Philadelphia, and enjoys an active life of sports — racquetball, tennis, golf, swimming and running. But his real vocation is working with high school students, telling them about Jesus Christ and the satisfying life which He offers.

# USE OF
# THIS MANUAL

**WHO ARE YOU, GOD?** is a study and discussion tool for individuals, one-on-one counselling, youth groups, weekend conferences, seminars and week-long camps.

**WHO ARE YOU, GOD?** is a teaching manual to challenge the thinking student who is looking for answers. It is an excellent resource for the youth leader who is seeking to develop the faith and commitment of students.

Scripture passages in this manual are highlighted to call attention to their importance and to make them stand out from the context. The Bible is our ultimate resource in life and is the heart of this study. Various versions are used to bring out the vital teaching of each passage and to communicate clearly what God says!

The questions are designed to motivate thoughtful discussion, make significant points clearly understandable and to apply Scripture to the individual in current experience.

The planned progression of this study makes it important for the youth leader and the student to follow the chapter topics in succession, at least for the first time. More intensive study of specific topics is recommended to bring out the full import of knowing God personally.

# CONTENTS

Foreword

Introduction ......................................................................1
1. FALSE IDEAS PEOPLE HAVE ABOUT GOD ................5
2. YOUR GOD MUST BE STRONG ..................................17
3. YOUR GOD MUST KNOW EVERYTHING .................27
4. YOUR GOD MUST BE BIG ..........................................39
5. YOUR GOD MUST BE IN CONTROL .......................47
6. YOUR GOD MUST BE HOLY.......................................57
7. YOUR GOD MUST BE LOVING ..................................67
8. YOUR GOD MUST BE MERCIFUL AND GRACIOUS..77
9. YOUR GOD MUST BE TRUSTWORTHY ....................89
10. YOUR GOD MUST BE A PERSON ...........................99
11. MAKE UP YOUR MIND............................................109

# FOREWORD

The abysmal ignorance of God that pervades our society today is shaping the future of our youth. It is understandable that natural man leaves God out of his thinking, but that those who claim to be believing Christians should be unable to express their concept of the living God is tragic.

The youth of today are being cheated, because no one is giving them the answers. Everywhere they look they face a vacuum concerning the intangible values of life and their own spiritual worth. The facts about God (which give substance to personal value) are either non-existent or unintelligible to their way of thinking.

Man is needy, helpless and despairing. Only a knowledge of the true God can help him. So it is vital that we listen to what God has revealed concerning Himself. Only as we learn about Him and what He is doing can we become the person He desires us to be.

**WHO ARE YOU, GOD?** challenges the inquiring student to discover the character of God and to apply that knowledge to his daily life. Such knowledge is vital — both for ourselves and for those around us.

The Publishers

# BUT YOU DO HAVE A GOD...

---

It is the nature of human beings to worship someone or something. Whether by default, indifference or neglect, everybody has a god! The Muslims worship Allah. The Jews worship Jehovah. Christians worship Jesus. The Hindus worship Buddha. Other cultures, nations, tribes and social groups have their idols, gods, voodoo relics and other objects of worship. In our day science and education are worshiped. Movie and television stars, sports heroes, political and even religious leaders are acclaimed with almost religious fanaticism, so that the downfall of one of these "gods" is a tragedy of widespread significance. Material things, such as cars, homes, business empires and wealth become idols that demand an excessive amount of time and devotion, even to the disruption and ruin of families and health. It doesn't matter which one or what you call it, but you have a god!

For some people there comes a specific time when they decide about their god, when they have an active opportunity to choose. Others never bother to think about their options. But the choice is always made, somehow, sometime. Everybody has a god!

The Bible begins with God, but the Bible also makes very clear that there are all sorts of substitutes and counterfeits. The God of the Bible declares Himself to be a God who acts, creates and controls. The prophet Isaiah spoke for God, saying:

> Isaiah 46:9 (NIV)
> *"I am God, and there is no other; I am God, and there is none like me."*

Hosea, in describing the character and work of God, spoke these words:

> Hosea 11:9 (NIV)
> *"For I am God, and not man"*

But the Bible does not hide the fact that there are all sorts of substitutes and counterfeits which men worship. Satan, in the Garden of Eden, persuaded Eve to believe him rather than God (and thus gained her worship). He took the place of God in man's thinking.

Household idols were carried by Rachel when she left her father's home. Jacob urged his household to put away the foreign gods which they owned. After making the gods of Egypt ridiculous, Moses had to warn his people and urge them to reject the gods of the land. Constantly, Israel fell prey to the idolatry of the nations and eventually went into exile because they rejected the God of their fathers and worshiped idols.

Mankind is faced with a choice: either honor the real God or find another. It is impossible to avoid the decision, though many will make their choice by omission. Mankind through the centuries has proven that he must have a god ... of some kind. The Bible begins by offering a knowledge of the real One, but each must decide for himself.

Joshua, that great leader of a small but significant group of Israelites, challenged his followers in the land of Canaan after they had successfully conquered the land which God gave to them. His charge to them was, "Choose ... this day whom you will serve" (Joshua 24:15). He and his family chose the living God!

EVERYBODY HAS A GOD!

# FALSE IDEAS PEOPLE HAVE ABOUT GOD

CHAPTER 1

There are no more important questions in all of life than "Is there a God?" and "What is He like?" The Bible is clear that God is not trying to hide from man or keep man confused as to His nature. But in spite of that, most men are terribly ignorant and confused about who the living and true God really is.

This confusion about what God is like has greatly affected the American teenager. The following are actual quotes from students asked to respond to the question, "What is God like?"

"A vague spirit that is everywhere."
"A ball of fire who loves you."
"He's kind of like Zeus — an old man in a toga."
"He loves me, I guess, but I see Him more as a commander."
"He is omnipotent, omniscient, omnipresent — if He exists."
"The old man upstairs."
"A being without form, without sex, but with a heart as big as the universe."
"God is my life."

How would you describe God? _____

_____

_____

_____

_____

Kind or cruel. Distant or near. Alive or dead. Everywhere or nowhere. Demanding or lenient. None of the above. All of the above. The choices are endless. Sometimes it seems like you're supposed to walk into the spiritual ice cream parlor and "build your own God." And this is actually what most people have done. Based on their own feelings about what God should be like, they have created their own god and have begun to worship it . . . or ignore it.

In this discussion, let us examine some of the many false ideas that people have concerning God.

## 1. THE MOST OBVIOUS FALSE IDEA ABOUT GOD IS THE BELIEF THAT THERE IS NO GOD AT ALL.

Most students are not atheists. In a recent survey, over 94% of all teenagers declared their belief in a higher being of some kind. Yet the belief that there is no God is aggressively proclaimed by a vocal minority.

But is there good evidence for believing in God's existence? The apostle Paul, in the book of Romans, gives us food for thought:

ROMANS 1:19,20 (TLB)

*For the truth about God is known to them instinctively: God has put this knowledge in their hearts. Since earliest times men have seen the earth and sky and all God made, and have known of his existence and great eternal power. So they will have no excuse.*

Based on Romans 1:19-20, why do you think so many teenagers believe in a higher being? _____

_____

_____

_____

In spite of the fact that God has revealed Himself to every person through His creation and through man's conscience, there are still those who reject the idea of God's existence. The writer of Psalms gives us a penetrating look into this type of person.

> PSALM 14:1-3 (NASB)
>
> *The fool has said in his heart, "There is no God." They are corrupt, they have committed abominable deeds; There is no one who does good. The Lord has looked down from heaven upon the sons of men, to see if there are any who understand, who seek after God. They have all turned aside; together they have become corrupt; there is no one who does good, not even one.*

In Psalm 14, what are the terms God Himself uses to describe the person who says He does not exist? _____

_____

_____

Why do you think atheists work hard to try and disprove God's existence? _____

_____

_____

Certainly it is the greatest of all insults to God to deny His existence and to seek to turn others from faith in Him. But those who reject Him do so, not from a lack of evidence, but from a heart that is unwilling to truly seek Him and submit to His rule in their lives. If there is a God, then as His created being, you are responsible to Him!

## 2. A SECOND FALSE IDEA ABOUT GOD IS THE BELIEF THAT GOD MAY EXIST, BUT CAN NEVER BE KNOWN.

The number of teenagers who would openly deny the existence of God is small. There is, however, a much more significant number of students that would say, "There may be a being or a spirit 'up there somewhere,' but it cannot be known personally." People who hold this view that God cannot be known personally are called agnostics.

It is abundantly plain that God does not force His attention on any of us, so getting to know Him takes some effort on our part. However, the agnostic or skeptic doesn't even want to bother trying, because he sees no value in knowing God anyway.

Job, a man of God from early times, gave a clear description of this type of person when he wrote:

> JOB 21:14-15 (NIV)
>
> *Yet they say to God, "Leave us alone! We have no desire to know your ways. Who is the Almighty that we should serve him? What would we gain by praying to him?"*

According to Job 21, the agnostic has deeper reasons than mere laziness for not seeking God. What are those reasons? _____

*To the agnostic ignorance is Bliss!*
*But God says ignorance is Death!*

_____

Jesus often dealt with crowds of people who, in reality, had no desire to know God, but enjoyed the miracles He performed and the food He fed them. He described these people in the following passage of Scripture:

> MATTHEW 13:14,15 (NASB)
>
> *"You will keep on hearing, but will not understand; and you will keep on seeing, but will not perceive; for the heart of this people has become dull, and with their ears they scarcely hear, and they have closed their eyes lest they should see with their eyes, and hear with their ears, and understand with their heart and return, and I should heal them."*

What was the condition of the people Jesus described in the passage above? ____

_____

_____

_____

Who did Jesus say was to blame for their condition? _____

_____

_____

The agnostic believes that it is not possible to know God and places the blame on God for not revealing Himself. However, this person has deceived himself. It is not that he *cannot* know God, but rather that he *will not* know God. To him, ignorance is bliss, when in reality, ignorance is death. The prophet Zechariah declared of them:

> **ZECHARIAH 7:11-12 (NIV)**
>
> *But they refused to pay attention; stubbornly they turned their backs and stopped up their ears. They made their hearts as hard as flint and would not listen to the law or to the words that the Lord Almighty had sent by his Spirit through the earlier prophets. So the Lord Almighty was very angry.*

## 3. ANOTHER FALSE IDEA ABOUT GOD IS THE BELIEF THAT GOD IS WEAK AND PERMISSIVE.

All of mankind faces a real dilemma when trying to understand God. The dilemma is simple. Deep within our heart of hearts, we realize that God is far more moral (holy) than we and we constantly do things that we know are wrong (sin). In order to deal with this problem, rather than turning from sin, many of us have painted a picture of God as being weak and permissive. This kind of foolish thinking gives rise to descriptions of God like:

"He's an old grandfather in a rocking chair in the sky, who shakes his tired head and shrugs his shoulders at the human race and says, 'Well, boys will be boys.'"

Somehow, the person who is caught up in immorality thinks and hopes that God is unaware of what he is doing. The prophet Isaiah set the record straight when he wrote:

> **ISAIAH 29:15-16 (TLB)**
> *Woe to those who try to hide their plans from God, who try to keep him in the dark concerning what they do! "God can't see us," they say to themselves. "He doesn't know what is going on!" How stupid can they be! Isn't he, the Potter, greater than you, the jars he makes? Will you say to him, "He didn't make us?" Does a machine call its inventor dumb?*

According to Isaiah 29, what do people do to try and

keep God from discovering their sin? _____

_____

From the Scripture above, what do men say to convince themselves that they have successfully tricked God?

_____

According to Isaiah, why are these self-deceptions absolutely foolish?

_____

_____

God is not weak. He sees all and knows all, even what is done in secret. And although some people hope that He does not see their sin, most realize that God does know. Therefore, to keep from turning from their evil ways, people have concocted a view of God that He is just like them, permissive and tolerant of sin. The Psalmist buried this notion that God doesn't care about evil when he wrote:

> PSALM 50:16-23 (NASB)
> *But to the wicked God says, "What right have you to tell of My statutes, and to take My covenant in your mouth? For you hate discipline, and you cast My words behind you. When you see a thief, you are pleased with him, and you associate with adulterers. You let your mouth loose in evil, and your tongue frames deceit. You sit and speak against your brother; you slander your own mother's son. These things you have done, and I kept silence; you thought that I was just like you; I will reprove you, and state the case in order before your eyes. Now consider this, you who forget God, lest I tear you in pieces, and there is none to deliver. He who offers a sacrifice of thanksgiving honors Me; and to him who orders his way aright I shall show the salvation of God."*

According to Psalm 50, what are the crimes against God of which the wicked

are guilty? _____

_____

_____

_____

How was the reasoning of the wicked faulty? _____

_____

Why did they think that God was permissive and lenient, just like

they were? _____

What did God say He would do to them if they did not turn away from their

wicked ways? _____

_____

_____

_____

_____

The significant truth about God is that He is just and loving. The terrible perversion of that truth is that God is lenient. He is not. He will judge sin. But since the creation of man, the enemy of our souls, Satan himself, has been lying to us. He has deceived us into thinking that God will not really punish sin. In Genesis, God clearly and lovingly warned Adam and Eve not to eat from the tree of the knowledge of good and evil. What was the punishment for disobedience of that command? Certain death! That's what God said. But Satan lied and told them:

> **Genesis 3:4 (NASB)**
> *"You surely shall not die!"*

The devil's strategy has not changed over the centuries. He is still telling the same lie. And countless people have swallowed that bait — hook, line and sinker. To achieve his own purposes, Satan seduces people by telling them that God does not really mean what He says. That is the big lie!

## 4. THE MOST POPULAR FALSE IDEA ABOUT GOD IS THAT HE IS AN ANGRY "COSMIC KILLJOY" DETERMINED TO MAKE LIFE MISERABLE.

At the opposite end of the spectrum are many people who don't see God as lenient or even loving at all. They are afraid of God and what He will do with their lives if they get to know Him.

Satan's deception of Eve in the Garden of Eden was masterful strategy. Not only did he convince her that God would not really punish her for disobedience, but he also attacked God's love and goodness. As Eve looked at the forbidden fruit, she marvelled at how nourishing it was, how delicious it looked and how wise she would become if she ate it. The devil saw his opening and remarked:

> **Genesis 3:5 (TLB)**
> *"God knows very well that the instant you eat it you will become like him, for your eyes will be opened - you will be able to distinguish good from evil!"*

Suddenly, God was no longer a good and generous Creator who had provided everything Adam and Eve could ever want or ever need. Now God was the cosmic killjoy, depriving them of something "wonderful." Surely God did not love them if He was keeping something from them!

The deception worked on Eve, and it has worked on countless millions of people since. Even Job himself, a "blameless and upright" man who "feared God and shunned evil" fell prey to this lie.

JOB 7:12-21 (TLB)
*"O God, am I some monster,*
*that you never let me alone? Even when I try to forget my misery in sleep,*
*you terrify with nightmares. I would rather die of strangulation than go on*
*and on like this. I hate my life. Oh, let me alone for these few remaining*
*days. What is mere man that you should spend your time persecuting*
*him? Must you be his inquisitor every morning, and test him every*
*moment of the day? Why won't you let me alone — even long enough to*
*spit? Has my sin harmed you, O God, Watcher of mankind? Why have*
*you made me your target, and made my life so heavy a burden to me?*
*Why not just pardon my sin and take it all away? For all so soon I'll lie*
*down in the dust and die, and when you look for me, I shall be gone."*

Job, undoubtedly, suffered much more than we ever have (see Job 1,2), so we ought not to be too quick to condemn him. But what were some of the things Job said which indicated he had begun to see God as cruel and angry?

_____

_____

_____

_____

_____

All of us at one time or another have questioned whether God really has our best interests in mind. It is so easy for us to fall into the popular notion that God is not dealing with us in love, but out of coldness and indifference.

Can you think of a time in your life when you felt God was unfair or cruel, like a "cosmic killjoy?" Briefly describe what happened.

_____

_____

The idea that God is a "cosmic killjoy" is almost as insulting to God as the assertion that He does not exist at all. God wants us to know that a life with Him in control will ultimately be the greatest life possible for us.

**IN CONCLUSION**

In this study, we have discussed just a few of the false ideas of what God is like. Nothing could be more devastating than to go through life and then face eternity without understanding what God is really like and how we can know Him.

The remainder of this discussion manual is designed to help you discover the true and living God and know whom you worship. The prophet Jeremiah summed up the loving invitation that God gives to all of us when he wrote:

> JEREMIAH 29:11-13 (TLB)
> *For I know the plans I have for you, says the Lord. They are plans for good and not for evil, to give you a future and a hope. In those days when you pray, I will listen. You will find me when you seek me, if you look for me in earnest.*

# YOUR GOD MUST BE STRONG

# CHAPTER 2

J B. Phillips wrote a book entitled *Your God Is Too Small*. Why do you think he felt the need to write a book with such a strange title? Certainly not because the God of the universe is *actually* small and weak, but because our *concept* of God is small and weak!

Someone once said, "God created man in His image, and then man returned the favor." Many of us have conjured up our own mental picture of God and then decided that this God is not worthy of our worship and trust.

One area of confusion about God deals with His greatness and power. How powerful is God? Is He threatened by our vast nuclear stockpiles, wishing that the good ol' days of bows and arrows were here? Or is He a powerful God who can snuff out a nuclear bomb as easily as if it were a candle?

The problem is that there are as many ideas of God's power as there are people on the street. Mere human opinion and speculation about God's strength will get us nowhere. We must go to God Himself and His revelation of what He is like — the Bible. The buck stops there. What Scripture says about God is true.

*WHAT DOES IT MEAN WHEN WE SAY THAT GOD IS OMNIPOTENT?*

God's power is His ability to act with total authority and strength to accomplish His purposes.

*THEREFORE, LET US TRY TO GET A GLIMPSE OF GOD'S POWER AND LEARN WHAT OUR RESPONSE TO IT SHOULD BE.*

## 1. GOD'S POWER IS SO AWESOME IT IS IMMEASURABLE.

It does not take long for our minds to be blown away when we contemplate the subject of power. Where does all strength come from and how much of it is there?

The Bible tells us that all power comes from God and that His might is without limit. The following verses will help us see this clearly.

> **PSALM 62:11 (NASB)**
> *Once God has spoken; twice I have heard this: that power belongs to God.*

> **GENESIS 17:1 (NASB)**
> *"I am God Almighty; walk before Me, and be blameless."*

According to Genesis 17:1, how much power belongs to God?

_____

_____

Scripture is clear that all power that has ever existed and has ever been used has come directly from God. From the strength of the tiny ant carrying its load, to the force unleashed in holding the stars in place, all power is from God.

In fact, God wants to make it very clear that He holds all power. Even His name declares it. "I am God Almighty," He says.

What do you think it means when we say that God has infinite power?

_____

_____

God's power is infinite. It has no limits in quantity, and no matter how much He uses, it can never be exhausted.

## THE "HOW POWERFUL IS GOD?" PROJECT:

Brainstorm and come up with some amazing things that an Almighty God can do.

For example, do you realize that God didn't really need six days to create the universe? He could have done it in an instant had He chosen to do so.

Or do you realize that God has the power to quench the fire of the sun and turn it into a gigantic snowball in less time than it takes to blink?

Do you know that the Almighty is so strong that He could destroy and re-create the universe an infinite number of times before we even knew what happened?

Have fun with this project, and remember that no matter how creative you are, God is able to do far beyond what you can ever imagine! (Just remember that God will not sin.)

_____

_____

_____

_____

_____

_____

_____

_____

_____

_____

Now that we have thought about how incredibly vast God's power is, we can understand why David wrote:

> PSALM 145:3 (NASB)
> *Great is the Lord, and highly to be praised; and His greatness is unsearchable.*

That says it all!

## 2. GOD'S POWER IS SO AWESOME NOTHING IS TOO DIFFICULT FOR HIM.

Sometimes we struggle so hard to accomplish the simplest tasks that we forget that God is not like us. He does not get tired or sick. He does not become depressed, lonely or frustrated. There is no task which causes Him to flinch.

In the project below, list some of the most physical, mental and emotionally-draining activities that you have engaged in. Include why each was so draining on you.

first week of football practice
_____

final exam in geometry
_____

_____

_____

_____

_____

_____

Unlike us, God has infinite power. Therefore, He is not bothered by tasks that would be impossible for us.

> JEREMIAH 32:17 (NASB)
> *"Ah Lord God! Behold Thou hast made the heavens and the earth by Thy great power and by Thine outstretched arm! Nothing is too difficult for Thee,"*

According to Jeremiah 32:17, what did God create? _____

_____

_____

According to the same passage, how was He able to do that?

_____

_____

Describe some of the parts of God's creation that are especially amazing to you.

Explain why you think it took so much power to create it. _____

_____

_____

_____

God rules the universe with complete ease. In fact, He has only to speak and His will is done.

PSALM 33:6,9 (TLB)
*He merely spoke, and the heavens were formed, and all the galaxies of stars. For when He but spoke, the world began! It appeared at his command!"*

*God can do far more with one word in an instant that all other created beings combined can do in all eternity.*

**LET THERE BE LIGHT!"**

According to Psalm 33, what was the only "tool" that God used in creating the universe?

_____

_____

_____

_____

What would happen to the universe if God spoke a word against it?

_____

_____

_____

We can speak and command others to work, but our words in and of themselves do nothing. But God's spoken word actually unleashes His incredible power!

**"GOD'S ANSWER TO MY PROBLEM" PROJECT**

Stop and think about what you've just learned of God's power and apply that knowledge to the problem you are facing right now.

In the spaces below, first list the struggles you are presently going through, then write down how you think God with His great power could solve them.

**PROBLEM**                                        **GOD'S SOLUTION**

_____              _____

_____              _____

_____              _____

_____              _____

_____              _____

Right now, before moving on, take a few moments and ask God in His infinite power to move into each situation and bring about His solution.

## 3. GOD'S POWER IS SO AWESOME NO ONE OR NOTHING CAN HINDER HIM.

Just because God is so overwhelmingly powerful does not mean that all created beings have obeyed God or have submitted to His great strength. The Bible tells us that Satan, his demonic forces and all those who do not turn to God try to resist Him. But all the forces of the universe combined in one effort cannot stop or even hinder what God purposes to do.

Job, that great man of God, understood this clearly after a personal visit from God Himself.

> JOB 42:2 (NIV)
> _"I know that you can do all things. No plan of yours can be thwarted."_

What are the most powerful forces, beings and things in the universe apart from God? Make a list:

_____ death _____ weather _____

_____

_____

_____

_____

_____

_____

What does Job 42:2 say that all these forces combined could do against God?

_____

_____

It is amazing to see how God responds to those who think they can stop Him from doing what He wants to do. In Psalm 2 we have a graphic picture of God's response to opposition.

*PSALM 2:1-5 (TLB)*
*What fools the nations are to rage against the Lord! How strange that men should try to outwit God! For a summit conference of the nations has been called to plot against the Lord and His Messiah, Christ the King. "Come, let us break his chains," they say, "and free ourselves from all this slavery to God." But God in heaven merely laughs! He is amused by all their puny plans. And then in fierce fury he rebukes them and fills them with fear."*

What are the attitudes and actions of those who hate God, according to Psalm 2?

_____

_____

_____

Why does God laugh at them? _____

_____

How do people respond when God pours forth His fierce anger upon them?

_____

_____

_____

The God of infinite power is not the least bit intimidated by the strongest, fiercest opposition His enemies can muster. He laughs for a moment, but in time turns His face against those who foolishly rage against Him.

## 4. GOD'S POWER IS SO AWESOME EVERYONE SHOULD PRAISE HIM.

All of us must constantly remind ourselves of the great power of God available for our lives. One of the best ways to remind ourselves is to get into the habit of worshipping, praising and trusting God for who He is, *no matter what!* The Bible says:

> PSALM 105:1-2 (NASB)
> *Oh give thanks to the Lord, call upon His name; make known His deeds among the peoples. Sing to Him, sing praises to Him; speak of all His wonders.*

As we have seen, God's power is truly mind-boggling. Take a few moments and review the main points of this chapter. Then in the space below write down two or three of the things about God's power that have impressed you most.

_____

_____

_____

_____

Now spend some time thanking God that He has revealed Himself as such a great and powerful God. Think about the following verse as you worship Him.

> ISAIAH 40:12 (TLB)
> *Who else has held the oceans in his hands and measured off the heavens with his ruler? Who else knows the weight of all the earth and weighs the mountains and the hills?*

## IN CONCLUSION

Even though you are but a speck in the dust of the universe - one among billions of creatures, God offers you His protection and tender care. The prophet Isaiah emphasized this when he said

> ISAIAH 42:3 (NIV)
> *A bruised reed he will not break, and a smoldering wick he will not snuff out.*

What a great privilege it is that the God who holds all the oceans of the world in the palm of His hand invites *us* to worship Him!

# CHAPTER 3

# YOUR GOD MUST KNOW EVERYTHING

I n our last discussion we caught a glimpse of God's power. We can never fully understand it, for how can we frail human beings ever grasp the total greatness of God? But we can understand enough to make us gaze in awe and wonder.

Now we turn to God's knowledge and wisdom. How much does He know? Is He baffled by our high tech, computer age? Does He scratch His head at the complexities of politics, economics and world affairs?

And what about our daily lives? Does He know anything about being a better athlete? Can He help us with our dating relationships? Does He know how we think and feel?

If God had all power but not all knowledge and wisdom, what kind of a God would He be? He would be incredibly strong, but prone to major blunders. If God knew everything but was not all powerful, what kind of God would He be? He would be a remarkably brilliant, yet terribly weak and frustrated God. Either way it would spell disaster for the human race.

*WHAT DOES IT MEAN THAT GOD IS OMNISCIENT?*

It means that God has such a great mind that He knows *everything about everything!*

*THEREFORE, LET US TRY TO GET A GLIMPSE OF THE EXTENT OF GOD'S KNOWLEDGE AND WISDOM, AND LEARN WHAT OUR RESPONSE SHOULD BE.*

## 1. GOD'S KNOWLEDGE IS SO VAST IT INCLUDES ALL THE DETAILS OF CREATION.

The universe seems so huge and outer space so deep, dark and cold that we often think that God is distant and impersonal. The following verse, penned by Isaiah, gives us a true glimpse of God's personal knowledge of His creation.

> ISAIAH 40:26 (TLB)
> *Look up into the heavens! Who created all these stars? As a shepherd leads his sheep, calling each by its pet name, and counts them to see that none are lost or strayed, so God does with stars and planets!*

In Isaiah 40:26, what does God do with all the stars and planets? _____

_____

_____

_____

_____

Do you have any idea how many stars there are in outer space? Astronomers tell us that there are billions and billions of galaxies, each having billions and billions of stars! And God knows all of them by name! Yet most of us struggle with remembering the names of everyone in our class at school!

But how much does God really know? The next scripture should give us some insight into that important questions.

> PSALM 147:5 (NASB)
> *Great is our Lord, and abundant in strength; His understanding is infinite.*

According to Psalm 147, how much does God know? _____

_____

_____

God knows everything. There is no speck of information, no piece of data that He cannot instantly and accurately bring to mind. That's way beyond genius. That's *all-knowing!* And that's God!

## THE "HOW MUCH DOES GOD KNOW" PROJECT:

Brainstorm and come up with some amazing things that an all-knowing God must know.

For example, do you realize that God knows the exact location and number of every single grain of sand on every beach in every country in the entire world?

Or do you know that if everyone of the 5 billion or so people on this planet decided to talk to God all at once, He would be able to hear each person and respond to each individual, *with no confusion, all at once!* Believe it . . . or not!

Now you try it. Come up with a couple of your own examples of God's incredible knowledge.

_____

_____

_____

_____

## 2. GOD'S KNOWLEDGE IS SO VAST IT INCLUDES ALL THE DETAILS OF MY LIFE.

It is an awe-inspiring experience to think about the extent of God's knowledge of the universe. It is sobering to think about the extent of God's knowledge of you and me! David spoke of this overwhelming thought in Psalm 139.

> PSALM 139:1-4 (TLB)
> *O Lord, you have examined my heart and know everything about me. You know when I sit or stand. When far away you know my every thought. You chart the path ahead of me, and tell me where to stop and rest. Every moment, you know where I am. You know what I am going to say before I even say it.*

According to Psalm 139, what are the areas of our lives that God knows completely?

_____

_____

_____

_____

What are some other areas of our lives not mentioned in this passage that God also understands completely? (For example, He knows what you will be doing after graduation.)

_____

_____

_____

_____

God knows our thoughts before we think them. He understands our emotions before we feel them. He anticipates our decisions long before we make them. He weeps, laughs, gets angry and smiles at our words long before we utter them. In fact, the following verses of Scripture say it best of all:

> HEBREWS 4:13 (TLB)
> *He knows about everyone, everywhere. Everything about us is bare and wide open to the all-seeing eyes of our living God; nothing can be hidden from him to whom we must explain all that we have done.*

> HOSEA 7:2 (NASB)
> *And they do not consider in their hearts that*
> *I remember all their wickedness. Now their deeds are all around them; they are before My face.*

How does it make you feel to know that everything you do is "bare and wide open to the all-seeing eyes of our living God?"

_____

_____

In what ways would your life be different if you were *constantly aware* that nothing can be hidden from God and that He sees all your wickedness?

_____

_____

Scripture tells us that God never gets tired or weary. He sees all, all the time. Like a piercing spotlight, His eyes probe the depths of our lives. He is never surprised and never confused. He never needs to be informed of what is happening.

As one Christian writer puts it:

"Though He be invisible to us, we are not so to Him. Neither the darkness of night, closed curtains, nor the deepest dungeon can hide any sinner from the eyes of Omniscience."

## GOD IS ALSO ALL-WISE

It is amazing to realize that God knows everything. But for God to be truly God He must be able to apply His knowledge to deal with the universe He has made. This includes our lives as well. Therefore, it is comforting to know that God is all-wise. In fact, the Bible says this about God:

> ROMANS 16:27 (TLB)
> *To God, who alone is wise, be the glory forever.*

## WHAT DOES IT MEAN THAT GOD IS ALL-WISE?

God's wisdom is His unique ability to take all that He knows and choose the purest and best means to accomplish His purpose.

The Bible tells us repeatedly that God does what He wants, when He wants, in the way He wants. Yet He never errs in all His actions, because God is full of wisdom. He knows the best way to accomplish all His plans.

## 3. GOD'S WISDOM IS SEEN IN CREATION.

It must have taken tremendous wisdom for God to create the universe. Think how much insight it must have taken to form the stars and work out the complexities of the universe.

The more we examine God's world, the more we marvel at His wisdom. The Bible talks about God's wisdom.

> PROVERBS 3:19 (NASB)
> *The Lord by wisdom founded the earth; by understanding He established the heavens.*

According to Proverbs 3:19, how did God create the earth?

_____

From what you know of God's power and wisdom, do you think it was difficult for God to create the universe? Why or why not?

_____

_____

The Scriptures say that God created the universe in six days. He did not *need* six days. He could have created everything in one instant, but He worked six days and rested on the seventh to give us an example to follow.

After each day's work, God stood back and looked at what He had done and saw that it was good. Because God is all-wise, all His creations are masterpieces. In fact, after God finished His work of creation, the Bible says that He saw that it was very good.

## THE "LOOK WHAT GOD DID IN HIS WISDOM" PROJECT

The book of Job records a great conversation between God and Job. Job, enduring tremendous suffering, began to question God and His dealings with him. God answered Job's doubts about divine wisdom by asking some questions about creation.

On the left side of the page is what God said to Job in this great encounter. Read these verses, then list on the right side of the page what God did in creation through His infinite wisdom.

### JOB 38:4-15 (TLB)                     WHAT GOD DID

*4 "Where were you when I laid the foundations of the earth? Tell me, if you know so much.*
*5 Do you know how its dimensions were determined, and who did the surveying?*
*6-7 What supports its foundations, and who laid its cornerstone, as the morning stars sang together and all the angels shouted for joy?*
*8-11 Who decreed the boundaries of the seas when they gushed from the depths? Who clothed them with clouds and thick darkness, and barred them by limiting their shores, and said, 'Thus far and no farther shall you come, and here shall your proud waves stop'?"*

Job felt utterly foolish that he had questioned God's wisdom, even though his suffering had been incredibly intense. Job got the message loud and clear. If God is the Master Architect of the universe, isn't He capable of handling our lives?

The Psalmist expresses the heart of what Job learned this way:

> PSALM 104:24 (NASB)
> *O Lord, how many are Thy works! In wisdom Thou hast made them all.*

## 4. GOD'S WISDOM IS SEEN IN MY BODY.

Another demonstration of the wisdom of God is seen in the intricate development of the human body. David himself spoke of it this way:

> Psalm 139:14 (TLB)
> *Thank you for making me so wonderfully complex! It is amazing to think about. Your workmanship is marvelous — and how well I know it.*

What was it about God's workmanship that moved David to thank God?

_____

_____

_____

_____

_____

_____

_____

_____

_____

From a couple of tiny, almost invisible cells your whole body has developed into a complicated but efficient masterpiece. Just think of the marvelous way in which your heart and lungs keep functioning all night long, even as you sleep.

Another aspect of God's wisdom is seen in the way cells operate within the body. Consider an example from the book *Fearfully and Wonderfully Made*, written by Dr. Paul Maier, that illustrates God's marvelous wisdom in creating the body. He describes the work of white blood cells responding to an emergency in the body:

"As if they have a sense of smell (we still don't know how they 'sense' danger), nearby white cells abruptly halt their aimless wandering. Like beagles on the scent of a rabbit, they home in from all directions to the point of attack. Using their unique shape-changing qualities, they ooze between overlapping cells of capillary walls and hurry through tissue via the most direct route. When they arrive, the battle begins."

"Like a blanket pulled over a corpse, the cells assume their (bacterial) shape; for awhile they still glow eerily inside the white cell. But the white cell contains granules of chemical explosives, and as soon as the bacteria are absorbed, the granules detonate, destroying the invaders. In thirty seconds to a minute only the bloated white cell remains. Often its task is a kamikaze one, resulting in the white cell's own death."

What is your response to the ideas which you have just read? What does this tell you about the wisdom of God?

_____

_____

_____

_____

_____

_____

_____

## IN CONCLUSION

What more can we say about God's knowledge and wisdom? It is far beyond all human comprehension. Yet what little we do understand of this God, who knows all and who does all things right, should move us to great praise. Then we can say with the apostle Paul,

ROMANS 11:33-36 (TLB)

*Oh what a wonderful God we have! How great are his wisdom and knowledge and riches! How impossible it is for us to understand his decisions and his methods! For who among us can know the mind of the Lord? Who knows enough to be his counselor and guide? And who could ever offer to the Lord enough to induce him to act? For everything comes from God alone. Everything lives by his power, and everything is for his glory. To him be glory evermore.*

# CHAPTER 4

# YOUR GOD MUST BE BIG

L oneliness is a terrible problem and a terrible feeling. Everyone experiences it at times in their life; thousands are experiencing it right now. And you don't have to be alone to be lonely. Even in a crowd at a football game or walking down the hall at school, you can feel isolated, alienated and alone.

Where does God fit in to all this? We have seen that He knows everything and can do whatever He wants, but is He there when you need Him? Is He there when you don't? Is He in heaven or on earth? Or both? Can we truly turn to Him at any time and know He's there?

It should be a great comfort to us to know that God is not limited by time and space. He exists outside of time and occupies all places at once. He is omnipresent.

*WHAT DOES IT MEAN THAT GOD IS OMNIPRESENT?*

God's omnipresence means literally that He is "all-present" or "present everywhere." He is present everywhere at every moment.

*LET US TAKE A LOOK AT GOD'S OMNIPRESENCE AND TAKE GREAT COMFORT IN KNOWING HE IS EVERYWHERE.*

## 1. GOD'S OMNIPRESENCE MEANS THAT HE IS EVERYWHERE.

When one of the Russian cosmonauts was traveling through space, he made the triumphant declaration that there could not be a God, because he had searched outer space and did not see him anywhere. Yet one of the writers of Psalms gives us another point of view, a true revelation from God Himself.

> PSALM 139:7-12 (TEV)
> *"Where could I go to escape from your spirit? Where could I get away from your presence? If I went up to heaven, you would be there; if I lay down in the world of the dead, you would be there.*
> *If I flew away beyond the east, or lived in the farthest place in the west, you would be there to lead me, you would be there to help me.*
> *If I could ask the darkness to hide me, or the light around me to turn into night, but even the darkness is not dark for you, and the night is as bright as the day.*
> *Darkness and light are the same to you."*

The writer of Psalm 139 discusses numerous places one could try to go where God is not. List them below.

_____

_____

_____

Where else do people mistakenly think they can go to avoid the presence of God? *example: not attending church on Sunday*

_____

_____

There is no place where one can go to escape the presence of Almighty God. He is in church with those who worship Him on Sunday and He is on the golf course with those who won't. He was with the American astronauts as they walked on the moon. And He was with the Russian cosmonaut who denied His existence.

Jeremiah the prophet spoke for God this way:

> JEREMIAH 23:23-24 (NASB)
> *"Am I a God who is near,"* declares the Lord, *"and not a God far off? Can a man hide himself in hiding places, so I do not see Him?"* declares the Lord. *"Do I not fill the heavens and the earth?"* declares the Lord.

If God is everywhere, you may ask, why is it that some people do not believe that He exists? Why would some people die for their belief in God, while others die laughing at those who believe? One reason is, though God is everywhere present, He is not everywhere visible. But how is it possible for one so great as Almighty God to seemingly go unnoticed by most of mankind?

## 2. GOD'S OMNIPRESENCE MEANS THAT HE IS AN INFINITE SPIRIT.

With very few exceptions, anywhere you travel on planet earth, you can find air. For the most part, you cannot see air. It is tasteless, colorless and odorless. But you know that air is all around you.

In much the same way, you cannot see God, but He is there. The following verses from the New Testament will help us understand the mystery of God's everywhere presence. The first passage is an account of Jesus' appearance to His disciples after rising from the dead.

LUKE 24:36-39 (NASB)
*And while they were telling these things, He Himself stood in their midst. But they were startled and frightened and thought that they were seeing a spirit. And He said to them, "Why are you troubled, and why do doubts arise in your hearts? See My hands and My feet, that it is I Myself; touch Me and see, for a spirit does not have flesh and bones as you see that I have."*

JOHN 4:24 (NASB)
*"God is spirit, and those who worship Him must worship in spirit and truth."*

In the Luke 24 passage, the disciples expressed alarm at seeing Jesus. Why?

_____

Jesus wanted His disciples to know He was not a spirit. What did He point out to convince them of this?

_____

_____

How does John 4:24 describe God? _____

What do you think it means that "God is spirit?" Describe in the space below, as best you can, what you think a spirit is.

_____

_____

Although we do not fully understand what a spirit is, we do know that it is invisible to the human eye. In 1 Timothy 6:16 we find further light on the mystery of God, the infinite spirit. He is declared to be the One —

> 1 TIMOTHY 6:16 (NASB)
> *Who alone possesses immortality and dwells in unapproachable light; whom no man has seen or can see.*

It can be a little confusing when we try to pinpoint where God actually is. Jesus instructed us to pray: "Our father, who art in heaven," yet Scripture also says that He is everywhere, not just in heaven. Perhaps the center or core of His being is in heaven, but He is too great and magnificent to be limited to one place, even a place as marvelous as heaven!

The following project is designed to help you gain a greater understanding of God's invisible omnipresence.

## THE "HOW CAN GOD BE EVERYWHERE" PROJECT

There are numerous things around us in our normal, everyday lives which to a lesser degree demonstrate the quality of being invisible yet present everywhere. We have already mentioned 'air' as one of those things. Do some creative brainstorming and come up with some others. Describe them in the spaces below.

_____ *light is invisible until it hits an object* _____

_____ *sound* _____

_____

_____

_____

_____

_____

[This is a picture of air]
↓

All the things around us that give us a glimpse of God's omnipresence are merely pictures, faint illustrations of the true God who is everywhere. But God is not a gas or a force or a ghost. He is a living, loving Person who, though holy and pure, seeks to draw us to Himself. And for those who truly seek to know Him, this is very good news!

## 3. GOD'S OMNIPRESENCE MEANS GREAT COMFORT FOR THOSE WHO KNOW AND LOVE HIM.

Since God is everywhere, we cannot travel where He is not or has not already been. He is around us and in us. He fills every nook and cranny of creation, from the farthest galaxy in outer space to the minutest cell of our body. He is indeed closer to us than our deepest sigh or faintest smile.

Each day has its joys and frustrations, times of happiness as well as times of pain. What a tremendous source of comfort it is to know that the God who knows and loves us walks with us through all these times. He is there to share the good times and He is there to help us through the tough times, as David beautifully reminds us:

---

PSALM 37:23-24 (NASB)
*The steps of a man are established by the Lord; and He delights in his way.*
*When he falls, he shall not be hurled headlong; because the Lord is the One who holds his hand.*

---

According to Psalm 37, man's steps are established by God. What do you think that means? _____

_____

_____

How does God feel about the life of a godly man? _____

_____

What does Psalm 37 say God does when we fall? Put David's thoughts into your

own words. Then express to God how this truth makes you feel. _____

_____

_____

_____

Like a loving and tender father leading his young child across a stream, our heavenly Father is with us to uphold and protect us when we slip. As Psalm 46 says,

> **PSALM 46:1 (NASB)**
> *God is our refuge and strength,*
> *a very present help in trouble.*

The apostle Paul declares that God wants men to:

> **ACTS 17:27 (NASB)**
> *Seek God, if perhaps they might grope for Him and find Him, though He is not far from each one of us.*

Though God is incredibly near to us, James reminds us that we must respond.

> **JAMES 4:8 (NASB)**
> *Draw near to God and He will draw near to you.*

## IN CONCLUSION

We often do not experience the presence of God, because we do not reach out to Him. Yet we can be confident that God is always there, ready and eager to spend time with us. We have a God who cares so much that He will *never* leave us.

> **HEBREWS 13:5-6 (NASB)**
> *Let your character be free from the love of money, being content with what you have; for He Himself has said, "I will never desert you, nor will I ever forsake you," so that we confidently say, "The Lord is my helper, I will not be afraid. What shall man do to me?"*

# CHAPTER 5

# YOUR GOD MUST BE IN CONTROL

I n our previous studies, we have begun to see Almighty God as He has revealed Himself in the Bible. We have seen that He is all-powerful. There is nothing He desires to do that He cannot do. We have also seen that God is all-wise and all-knowing. There is nothing He does not know, and all He does is done in the best way possible. But we have only begun. There is much more to be said about the greatness of God. He not only does all and knows all, but He is also absolutely sovereign.

*WHAT DOES IT MEAN THAT GOD IS SOVEREIGN?*

God's sovereignty is His absolute over all that exists and over all that takes place everywhere.

*LET US TAKE A LOOK AT WHAT IT MEANS THAT GOD IS IN TOTAL CONTROL AND LEARN WHAT OUR RESPONSE TO HIS SOVEREIGNTY SHOULD BE.*

## 1. GOD'S SOVEREIGNTY MEANS THAT HE ALONE ALWAYS HAS THE FREEDOM TO DO WHATEVER HE CHOOSES.

"Freedom," like "love," is a word that is often used and often misused in our society. There are nearly as many definitions of freedom as there are people.

How would you define *personal* freedom? _____

_____

_____

_____

Some people define personal freedom as being able to do whatever they want. But what happens if what *you* want to do conflicts with what *I* want to do? Whose freedom wins out? And what happens when our freedom runs up against a natural law, such as gravity? Mankind is really not free to do what he wants!

And what about God? Does He deal with these kinds of conflicts? The Bible shows us that God's freedom to do what He wants goes far beyond anything that man can do or even dream of doing. David referred to God's freedom this way:

> PSALM 115:2-3 (NASB)
> *Why should the nations say, "Where, now,*
> *is their God?" But our God is in the heavens; He does whatever He pleases.*

According to Psalm 115, what does God have freedom to do?

_____

If every person had the kind of freedom that God has, what would the world be like? Explain your answer:

_____

_____

Based on what we have discussed so far in the previous chapters, would you say it is "good news" or "bad news" to know that God "does whatever He pleases." Explain your answer:

_____

_____

_____

_____

God is in absolute, total control of all that goes on in the universe. That is, God is at every time, in every place, *free* to do as He pleases. But God is not selfish and short-sighted like we are, therefore He never abuses His freedom. He seeks permission from no one, for who is greater than He? He can be stopped by no one, for who is more powerful than He?

## 2. GOD'S SOVEREIGNTY MEANS THAT NO ONE CAN OVERRULE HIM.

Each day's news brings chilling stories of the evil plans of various heads of nations and terrorist leaders. The world seems to be tottering on the edge of a major conflict with all-out nuclear war. It is easy to wonder where God is in all this mess.

Even though current events are alarming, God's Word brings comforting news.

> 1 TIMOTHY 6:15-16 (NASB)
> *He who is the blessed and only Sovereign, the King of kings and Lord of lords; who alone possesses immortality and dwells in unapproachable light, whom no man has seen or can see. To Him be honor and eternal dominion! Amen.*

From 1 Timothy 6:15-16, list the words and phrases that describe God as the One who is in ultimate control.

_____

_____

What do you think it means that God is "King of kings and Lord of lords?"

_____

_____

_____

God is described as the "*only* sovereign." What would be the outcome in the universe if God had only partial control and someone else had the rest?

_____

_____

What does it mean that God has "eternal dominion?" Why is this comforting

to know? _____

_____

_____

   God is the *only* Sovereign. He shares control of the universe with no one. No man, woman, angel or devil can rise up to seize His throne. Satan thought he could, but he failed. Men think they can, but they are only kidding themselves. All those who call themselves kings and lords will one day bow in worship to the One who is the King of all kings and Lord of all lords, God Almighty! And how long will He rule? His dominion is *eternal*! It will never end.

   The mighty nations of the world have the nuclear capacity to destroy all life on earth several times over. They have the capability of sending spacecraft rocketing to the outer reaches of the solar system, billions of miles away. Is God impressed with all this? Let's see what God says about the nations of the world.

> ISAIAH 40:15,17 (NASB)
> *Behold, the nations are like a drop from a bucket, and are regarded as a speck of dust on the scales; behold, He lifts up the islands like fine dust. All the nations are as nothing before Him, they are regarded by Him as less than nothing and meaningless.*

Describe the nations of the world as God sees them.

_____

_____

_____

Based upon the truths about God from this chapter and the preceding ones, why

do you think God is not intimidated by any nation? _____

_____

_____

In the light of Isaiah 40:15,17, how should we react when news of threatening

wars and conflicts scream at us through the news media? _____

_____

God does not even blink an eye when the mightiest nations of the world rise up against one another. He is no more alarmed by them than by a drop of water sliding down the outside of a bucket. The nations are mere "drips" before God. And since God is in control and does not fear them, we shouldn't fear them either.

The prophet Isaiah goes on to describe how the Bible views the mightiest ruler of the world.

> ISAIAH 40:22-23 (NASB)
> *It is He who sits above the vault of the earth, and its inhabitants are like grasshoppers, Who stretches out the heavens like a curtain and spreads them out like a tent to dwell in. He it is who reduces rulers to nothing, Who makes the judges of the earth meaningless.*

According to Isaiah 40, how does God view the inhabitants and leaders of the

world? _____

_____

When a new president is elected or a new judge is appointed, what does this

passage say is *really* happening _____

_____

It is exciting to see the world through God's eyes. We realize that because God is sovereign, *nothing* happens by chance or "accident." But it does not take long to begin to wonder why, if God *is* in control, the world is in the mess it is.

## 3. GOD'S SOVEREIGNTY DOES NOT MEAN THAT HIS WILL IS ALWAYS DONE ON EARTH.

Well over a million unborn children are murdered each year in America in a legalized slaughter called abortion. Six million Jews were incinerated in the gas ovens of Nazi Germany during World War II. These and a thousand more atrocities throughout history make it clear that God does *not* impose His will upon man. In fact, every time we sin, we defy God's sovereign rulership over the world and over our lives.

Why doesn't God intervene and stop all evil? He is sovereign and possesses all power, so He could if He chose to do so. But why doesn't He? Such questions have puzzled mankind for centuries.

The Bible clearly teaches that much of

man's suffering is due to his own wilful disobedience of a sovereign God. Before his death, Moses reminded the people of Israel about God's conditions for their well-being. Those principles are still applicable today.

DEUTERONOMY 30:17-20 (NASB)
*"But if your heart turns away and you will not obey, but are drawn away and worship other gods and serve them, I declare today that you shall surely perish. You shall not prolong your days in the land where you are crossing the Jordan to enter and possess it. I call heaven and earth to witness against you today, that I have set before you life and death, the blessing and the curse. So choose life in order that you may live, you and your descendants, by loving the Lord your God, by obeying His voice, and by holding fast to Him; for this is your life and the length of your days."*

According to Deuteronomy 30, what is the reason why there is so much death and misery in the world? _____

_____

_____

_____

_____

If the Lord is the only true God (and He is), what does Moses mean when he warns us against worshiping and serving "other gods?" _____

_____

_____

_____

_____

What must we do to bring God's blessings and avoid God's curses upon our land and upon ourselves? _____

_____

_____

_____

God, in His infinite wisdom, has sovereignly chosen to give man the option to obey or disobey Him. For the most part we have turned to the "gods" of material possessions, selfish ambitions, success, sports and relationships, instead of turning to God Himself. Whenever we put anyone or anything at the center of our lives, it becomes our god. And God says we will suffer the consequences of our evil ways.

We would be giving false information if we made it seem like *all* our problems were a direct result of our *own* sin. This is not the case. However, all suffering occurs because we live in a sin-filled world which lies under the judgment of Almighty God. So, even though bad things happen to good people, there is good news!

## THE "GOD IS IN CONTROL" PROJECT

Make a list of things which God controls and which man can do little to change:

| THING | ACTIVITY | RESULT IF GOD QUIT |
|---|---|---|
| *heart* | *blood supply* | *death* |
| *gravity* | *stability* | *spin off into space* |
| | | |
| | | |
| | | |
| | | |
| | | |
| | | |

God is truly in control. When things seem hopeless and evil things happen to us, God is still on His throne. He is still able to turn evil to His good purposes, as the apostle Paul states in Romans 8.

> ROMANS 8:28-29 (TLB)
> *And we know that all that happens to us is working for our good if we love God and are fitting into his plans. For from the very beginning God decided that those who came to him — and all along he knew who would — should become like his Son, so that his Son would be the First, with many brothers.*

According to Romans 8, is *everything* that happens to us good?

_____

_____

_____

God never promised that everything that happens to us would be good. But, according to this passage, what is God able to do with the bad things that occur in our lives?

_____

_____

_____

God *does* promise to turn *evil* to His good purpose. But to whom does this

promise apply? _____

_____

_____

What does Romans 8:28-29 say is God's ultimate purpose for His children?

_____

_____

_____

God in His sovereign wisdom sometimes chooses to sacrifice our temporary happiness in order to make us more like His Son, the Lord Jesus Christ. If Jesus "learned obedience through the things which He suffered" (Heb 5:8), why should it surprise us that sometimes *we* need to suffer in order to learn to obey?

God is all-knowing and all-wise. He knows the best plan of action. God is all-powerful. He is able to carry out His plans. God is absolutely, always, sovereignly free. No one can overrule Him.

Therefore we should not fear when the world situation is in chaos. Behind the scenes, God is still in control. Nor should we panic when our personal lives seem to go haywire. God is on His throne!

No wonder Nebuchadnezzar was so greatly humbled when he saw a sovereign God in action. This mighty king of Babylon confessed:

DANIEL 4:34-35 (NASB)
*"For His dominion is an everlasting dominion, and His kingdom endures from generation to generation. And all the inhabitants of the earth are accounted as nothing, but He does according to His will in the host of heaven and among the inhabitants of earth; and no one can ward off His hand or say to Him, 'What hast Thou done?'"*

## IN CONCLUSION

We are persuaded, from the evidence which the Bible records, that God is sovereign. He runs everything; He is Boss! And because He is, He deserves our obedience and submission to His will. It is really foolish for us to think and act as if we can overrule or overcome His authority. God has His rights and we need to recognize them.

But we also should submit to Him, because everything He controls and does is for our best interests. The sovereign God has us at the center of His thoughts and actions. Everybody who ever lets God run his life finds this is true!

# YOUR GOD MUST BE HOLY

We have taken a look in the last five chapters at the marvelous abilities God possesses. He can do anything. He knows everything. He is everywhere. He is in total control of all that goes on. These are enough to fill us with awe.

But what of God's character? What is He like? How does He view the world and what goes on in it? How does He view you and me and what we think and do? Some of these questions can be answered by discovering God's holiness.

There are certain words that you hear in church or see in the Bible that create a picture in your mind, even if you are not exactly sure what those words really mean . . . words like "saint" and "spiritual" and "grace." The term "holy" is such a word for many people.

Would you consider it a compliment, if someone called you a holy person? Why

or why not? _____

_____

_____

Whether you can see any benefit in the title of "holy" or not, that is the one given to God. His holiness is one of the most amazing of His attributes.

*WHAT IS THE HOLINESS OF GOD?*

To say that God is holy means that He possesses absolute moral purity and separation from all that is evil.

*SINCE THE HOLINESS OF GOD IS SO IMPORTANT, LET US EXAMINE WHAT IT MEANS THAT GOD IS HOLY AND DETERMINE WHAT EFFECT THAT SHOULD HAVE ON OUR LIVES.*

## 1. GOD IS SO HOLY THAT HE IS SEPARATED FROM ALL EVIL.

That great Old Testament prophet, Isaiah, helps us understand more clearly the awesomeness of God when he writes:

> ISAIAH 57:15 (NIV)
> *For this is what the high and lofty One says — he who lives forever, whose name is holy: "I live in a high and holy place, but also with him who is contrite and lowly in spirit, to revive the spirit of the lowly and to revive the heart of the contrite."*

How is God described in Isaiah 57:15? List below the words and phrases that

give you a picture of what He is like. _____

_____

_____

_____

God is referred to as "the high and lofty One." Our first response is to think this refers to His being in heaven, high up in the sky somewhere. In what other sense

could God be called "high and lofty?" _____

_____

_____

_____

_____

_____

Does God, according to Isaiah 57:15, remain high above and separated from

everyone? Explain your answer. _____

_____

_____

_____

God is holy. He is infinitely high and great and separated from sin and sinful men. He has a perfect shield of purity that surrounds Him, permitting no evil in His presence — without exception.

But the beauty of God in His perfect holiness is that He will live with those who are broken-hearted over their sin. When a person recognizes that he has sinned against a holy and righteous God, mourns over it, turns from it and seeks forgiveness, God in His kindness and mercy reaches down and cleanses him.

Therefore we see that God is holy. He is in a class by Himself. He is infinitely above the best that man can produce.

## 2. GOD IS SO HOLY THAT HE CAN NEITHER SIN NOR BE TEMPTED TO SIN.

We, who so easily disobey God and so often enjoy our sin, find it hard to relate to someone who does not want to join in our rebellion. God will never hop on the "sin bandwagon" with us. Never! The following verse helps us see that.

> 1 JOHN 1:5 (NASB)
> *And this is the message we have heard from Him and announce to you, that God is light, and in Him there is no darkness at all.*

The Bible says that God is light. What does 1 John 1:5 mean when it says,

"God is light?" _____

_____

According to 1 John, in God "there is no darkness at all." What do you think that

means? _____

_____

_____

All through the Bible, light is a symbol for moral purity and holiness. Darkness is a symbol for evil and sin. Notice that 1 John 1:5 does not say that God is bright or that He shines. No, it says He *is* light itself. In other words, God is not merely morally good and pure. He is purity and sinlessness itself. His brilliant purity outshines the sun as a laser outshines a dying ember. In fact, in heaven there will be no need for the sun or moon, for God Himself will illuminate it by the brilliance of His being.

## THE "GOD IS LIGHT" PROJECT

It is no accident that John used the term "light" to describe God in His holiness. In the spaces below, list some of the things that light does, as well as the qualities that light possesses. Relate those things to God in His holiness.

| PHYSICAL LIGHT | THE HOLINESS OF GOD |
|---|---|
| *travels through smog, but* | *is not corrupted by world's sin* |
| *does not get dirty* | *destroys sin* |
| *dispels darkness* | |
| | |
| | |
| | |
| | |
| | |
| | |
| | |

It should not come as a surprise that God is sinless. Unlike the old Greek gods of mythology, who had as many problems as men, our God does not sin and cannot sin. In fact, God is so holy that He cannot even be tempted to sin.

> JAMES 1:13 (NASB)
> *Let no one say when he is tempted, "I am being tempted by God;" for God cannot be tempted by evil, and He Himself does not tempt any one.*

According to James 1:13, what two things will never happen with God? _____

_____

The wonder of the holiness of God is that He, having no evil desire, is incapable of even being *tempted* to sin! The most alluring and enticing thing that the cunning mind of Satan conjures up does not phase God one bit. He is holy!

### 3. GOD IS SO HOLY THAT HE HATES SIN.

It is surprising to many people that God hates anything. We have heard for so long that "God is love" (as indeed He is), but we have forgotten that "God is holy." God's love is a holy love and, because God is holy, He cannot ignore or tolerate sin, much less like it. He is never lenient toward sin. Sin deeply offends God and He hates it, as the following verses make clear.

> PROVERBS 6:16-19 (NIV)
> *There are six things the Lord hates, seven that are detestable to him: haughty eyes, a lying tongue, hands that shed innocent blood, a heart that devises wicked schemes, feet that are quick to rush into evil, a false witness who pours out lies and a man who stirs up dissension among brothers.*

Proverbs 6 mentions seven things that God hates. List them in the space below, putting each into your own words:

_____

_____

_____

_____

_____

_____
_____
_____
_____
_____
_____

It should shake us up to realize how often we think, say and do things that God hates. How often we lie, tell half-truths and exaggerate something to look good. God hates that. How often we lay awake thinking of ways to hurt people, to gain revenge or to use people sexually! God hates that. How often we cut others down, gossip and cause friction in our families! God hates that, too. In fact, our sin is a stench in the nostrils of God.

## 4. GOD IS SO HOLY THAT ONE DAY HE WILL WIPE OUT ALL SIN AND ITS CONSEQUENCES.

Man's sin has not only corrupted man himself, but the entire universe as well. Although Christ's work on the cross has dealt a death blow to sin in the lives of those who turn to Him for forgiveness, the world around us will not be so fortunate. The following verses show how serious God is about wiping out sin and its effects forever.

> 2 PETER 3:10-13 (NASB)
> *But the day of the Lord will come like a thief, in which the heavens will pass away with a roar and the elements will be destroyed with intense heat, and the earth and its works will be burned up. Since all these things are to be destroyed in this way, what sort of people ought you to be in holy conduct and godliness, looking for and hastening the coming of the day of God, on account of which the heavens will be destroyed by burning, and the elements will melt with intense heat! But according to His promise we are looking for new heavens and a new earth, in which righteousness dwells.*

According to 2 Peter 3, what does God plan to do with the present universe (the heavens and the earth)?

_____

_____

_____

Why do you think such drastic measures will be necessary?

_____

_____

How does this scripture passage help you to get a clearer grasp of the

holiness of God? _____

_____

_____

According to these verses, what will be the primary characteristic of the new
heavens and the new earth?

_____

In light of what God plans to do with this present universe, what should your

attitude toward sin be? _____

_____

_____

Rarely do we realize how horrible it is to offend God's holiness. Too often we
are more concerned about offending our friends than we are about offending God.
Sin dishonors God. It was sin that sent Jesus to the cross and caused Him to give
His life for us. And sin is what eventually kills us as well. In fact, sin is so
abhorrent to God that our world, as we know it, is contaminated beyond repair by
man's moral impurity. To rid the universe of this terrible plague called sin, God has
decided to create a whole new heavens and earth where people will do
what is right.

## IN CONCLUSION

God longs to show His love toward us, but because He is holy we must first
come to Him on *His* terms to receive cleansing from our sin. Then He calls us to
a life of purity, urging us to turn from sin and learn to hate it as He does. Although
He is always ready to forgive us as we humbly confess our sins, God says with all
intensity:

> 1 PETER 1:14-16 (TLB)
> *Obey God because you are his children; don't slip back into your old
> ways — doing evil because you knew no better. But be holy now in
> everything you do, just as the Lord is holy, who invited you to be his
> child. He Himself has said, "You must be holy, for I am holy."*

An impossible task? How can God expect us to be holy as He is holy? Simply, because God has given the Holy Spirit to those who are truly His followers. By depending on Him for strength to say "no" to sin, you will find the power to obey.

God is holy. You can be, too . . . if you truly want to be.

# CHAPTER 7

# YOUR GOD MUST BE LOVING

hen most people think about God, they think of His love. Yet few people really understand what God's love is really all about. The Bible tells us much about God's love, but what exactly is it? In this chapter we will discuss what God's love is like, but first let's define it.

*WHAT IS GOD'S LOVE?*

The love of God is His intense desire and commitment to shower deep affection and complete self-sacrifice upon all mankind.

*LET US SEEK TO UNDERSTAND WHAT GOD'S LOVE IS LIKE, HOW IT IS EXPRESSED AND WHAT OUR RESPONSE SHOULD BE.*

## 1. GOD IS SO LOVING BECAUSE ALL LOVE ORIGINATES FROM HIM.

God is much greater than man could ever be. It should not surprise us, then, to find that His love is as high above man's love as the heavens are above the earth. One way in which God's love differs from man's is in its origin.

There is nothing more wonderful in our lives than love. But we may wonder where all this love comes from. The Bible states clearly that all love comes from God.

1 JOHN 4:7-8 (NASB)
*Beloved, let us love one another, for love is from God; and every one who loves is born of God and knows God. The one who does not love does not know God, for God is love.*

According to 1 John 4, where does all love come from?

_____

The Bible says that "God is love." What do you think that means? _____

_____

The Bible affirms that God is not merely loving, He _is_ love. Love is His very nature and all that He is and does overflows with it. Yet none of God's qualities are contradictory. He expresses all His attributes at the same time, all the time. His love is a holy love, a wise love, a powerful love and an unchanging love.

All love comes from God. Therefore, all the love we experience on a daily basis is a reminder of His commitment to us. And, though human expressions of love are not perfect, they can be pictures pointing us to God's deep affection for us.

The following project is designed to help us see how God's love is reflected in our world.

## THE "GOD'S LOVE IN THE WORLD" PROJECT:

Many times during the day we see acts of love and fail to recognize that God is the ultimate source of that love. In the space provided, list all the things you can think of that people do which communicate a touch of God's love.

_a mother tenderly holding her baby_

_a father scolding his child for running into the street_

_____

_____

_____

_____

_____

As beautiful as human displays of love can be, there is nothing like the love God has for us. We are frail and our love is weak, but God's love, like an infinite reservoir, knows no bounds.

## 2. GOD IS SO LOVING, BECAUSE HIS LOVE IS EVERLASTING AND LIMITLESS.

The idea of infinity staggers our minds. We cannot comprehend it. But such is God's love. God's love is so awesome that He is able to love all five billion people in the world at the same instant and for all eternity, without depleting His supply of love one bit!

In a song of praise to God for all His goodness, love and strength, David spoke of the greatness of God's love when he wrote:

PSALM 103:11,17 (NASB)
*For as high as the heavens are above the earth, so great is His loving kindness toward those who fear Him.*
*But the loving kindness of the Lord is from everlasting to everlasting on those who fear Him.*

According to Psalm 103, how great is God's love? Explain it in your

own words. _____

_____

Verse 17 says that "the lovingkindness of the Lord is from everlasting to everlasting." What do you think that means?

_____

_____

According to these verses, to what people do these promises of God's everlasting and limitless love apply?

_____

To those who embrace Jesus Christ as their Savior and Lord, there is the promise of the eternal outpouring of God's love upon them, no matter what happens in this life.

**69**

The apostle Paul wrote of this great promise when he penned some of the most comforting words in all Scripture:

ROMANS 8:38-39 (TLB)
*For I am convinced that nothing can ever separate us from his love. Death can't, and life can't. The angels won't, and all the powers of hell itself cannot keep God's love away. Our fears for today, our worries about tomorrow, or where we are — high above the sky, or in the deepest ocean — nothing will ever be able to separate us from the love of God demonstrated by our Lord Jesus Christ when he died for us.*

List in the space below all the things Paul mentions in Romans 8:38-39 that can never separate us from God's love.

_____

_____

_____

Can you think of anything else or anyone who might try to steal God's love from us? If so, list them below.

_____

_____

_____

Why is it impossible for *anything* to separate us from God's love?

_____

_____

Because God is all-powerful, when He chooses to love someone, no one can stop Him — no one is greater than He. Because God is so great, when He promises to do something He always comes through. And to show us He really loved us, He gave us His Son, Jesus, as a demonstration of that love.

### 3. GOD IS SO LOVING, BECAUSE HE LOVE IS SACRIFICIAL AND LOYAL.

Unfortunately, much of what we call love is shallow and self-centered. God's love is not like that! He always seeks to *give* rather than *get*.

Prior to His death, the Lord Jesus spoke of what true love was really like and how to recognize it. His disciples were unaware, when Jesus spoke, that He would demonstrate this very love within a few days.

> JOHN 15:13 (NASB)
> *"Greater love has no one than this, that one lay down his life for his friends."*

In John 15:13, what did Jesus say was the supreme act of love? _____

_____

God could someday ask us to give up our lives for those we love. Until then, however, what are some of the ordinary ways in which we can give of ourselves to our friends?

_____

_____

_____

To lay down your life for a friend is a beautiful act of sacrificial love. But God's love goes even beyond that. God Himself came to earth in the person of Christ to die for those who *hated* Him, His enemies! The apostle Paul wrote of such marvelous love this way:

> ROMANS 5:6-8 (NASB)
> *For while we were still helpless, at the right time Christ died for the ungodly. For one will hardly die for a righteous man; though perhaps for the good man someone would dare even to die. But God demonstrates His own love toward us, in that while we were yet sinners, Christ died for us.*

According to Romans 5, for what kind of person will a man perhaps die?

_____

_____

_____

For what kind of people did Jesus Christ die?

_____

_____

_____

In the light of previous discussions in this manual, why is it remarkable that Christ died for sinners like you and me?

_____

_____

_____

How many people would you be willing to die for? List them in the space below and explain briefly why?

_____

_____

_____

If the truth were known, most of us would not die for anyone. And those we might give our lives for would probably be family, friends or others we respect. Very few of us would die for our worst enemy. But that is exactly what God did, because sin made us all enemies of God!

Jesus' death on the cross means we no longer have to wonder how much God loves us. He didn't just say, "I love you," He showed it. And for all eternity the nailprints in His hands and feet will be a constant reminder of God's love for us.

"But that was almost 2,000 years ago," you say. "How does God show His love for me today, right now when I need someone to talk to?" It should encourage us greatly to know that God is a friend who loves at all times.

Imagine for a moment a friend who would never move away, never desert you, never cut you down, never talk about you behind your back and would always think and do the best for you. What a friend!

God is such a friend. He delights in us and thoroughly enjoys spending time with us. David knew God as a loyal friend.

PSALM 139:17-18 (TLB)
*How precious it is , Lord, to realize that you are thinking about me constantly! I can't even count how many times a day your thoughts turn toward me. And when I waken in the morning, you are still thinking of me!*

According to Psalm 139, what is one of the ways God shows His loyal friendship

to us? _____

_____

_____

How does it make you feel to realize God is constantly thinking loving

thoughts about you? _____

_____

_____

_____

It is good to have a friend who thinks about you a lot. It is even more wonderful to have a friend who sticks with you no matter what. God is a friend like that. The writer of Hebrews tells us how close God sticks to us.

HEBREWS 13:5 (NASB)
*He Himself has said, "I will never desert you, nor will I ever forsake you."*

What does God promise He will never do in Hebrews 13:5?

_____

Do you think God will leave you when you sin? _____

Why not? _____

How does it make you feel to know that God is a friend you can count on forever? In the space below, write a brief note to God, expressing your feeling to Him.

_____

_____

_____

_____

_____

_____

## 4. GOD'S LOVE MOTIVATES US TO LOVE HIM AND OTHERS.

We have seen very clearly that God's love is much higher and purer than man's love. He is constantly giving of Himself in deep affection and loyal friendship. Yet, impossible as it may seem, God expects His children to show His kind of love back to Him and to others. In fact, Jesus said there was no more important thing for us to do than to love God and others.

MATTHEW 22:37-39 (TLB)
*Jesus replied, "Love the Lord your God with all your heart, soul and mind. This is the first and greatest commandment. The second most important is similar: Love your neighbor as much as you love yourself."*

Only God Himself is able to give you the strength to love in the way Jesus wants you to. The following project will help you recognize when you are loving with God's supernatural love and when you are not.

### THE "LOVING WITH GOD'S LOVE" PROJECT:

In the left-hand column below are listed some of the qualities of God's love as found in 1 Corinthians 13:4-8. In the right-hand column, describe how man's limited love contrasts with God's pure love.

| GOD'S LOVE | MAN'S LOVE |
|---|---|
| Patient with annoying people | Impatient when tired, annoyed |
| Kind to those who hate you | |
| Never jealous or possessive | |
| Never boastful or arrogant | |
| Never demands its own way | |
| Forgiving, holds no grudge | |
| Loyal no matter what | |
| Believes the best in others | |
| Endures all kinds of hurts | |
| Always glad about the truth | |
| Never gives up on others | |

## IN CONCLUSION

We have caught only a glimpse of the love of God, but even a glimpse can be life changing. And were we to spend the rest of our lives in its pursuit, we could never fully fathom the depths of the love of God, for God is love.

EPHESIANS 3:17-19 (TLB)
*May your roots go down deep into the soil of God's marvelous love; and may you be able to feel and understand, as all God's children should, how long, how wide, how deep, and how high his love really is; and to experience this love for yourselves, though it is so great that you will never see the end of it or fully know or understand it. And so at last you will be filled up with God himself.*

# YOUR GOD MUST BE MERCIFUL AND GRACIOUS

# CHAPTER 8

I n our last discussion, we began to probe the depths of God's marvelous love. There is nothing more beautiful to know and experience than the love of God. And this is one of God's great desires. He wants us to experience this love for ourselves, though it is so great that we will never experience the end of it or fully know and understand it.

We have also observed that God is a holy and just God. He hates sin and will by no means leave the guilty unpunished. Although He is never lenient with sin, God is not a raging, seething tyrant. God has a tender heart, longing to pour out His compassionate love on mankind.

In this discussion, we will examine God's mercy - probably one of the most misunderstood of His attributes - and His grace, the ultimate expression of His character.

*WHAT IS THE MERCY OF GOD?*

God's mercy is His tender compassion for all His creatures and His willingness to withhold punishment for those deserving of judgment.

*WHAT IS THE GRACE OF GOD?*

The grace of God is that free gift of eternal life to those deserving nothing but judgment.

*LET US THEREFORE SEEK TO COMPREHEND THE MERCY AND GRACE OF GOD AND LEARN WHAT OUR RESPONSE TO THEM SHOULD BE.*

**1. GOD IS MERCIFUL TO ALL HIS CREATURES, EVEN THE UNGRATEFUL.**

Though we live in a cruel and unjust world where suffering is rampant, God's hand of mercy is all around us. Were God to allow people and their environment to experience the full effect of mankind's sin, we would all be destroyed.

Without realizing it, the human race receives countless gifts of mercy from God each day. But God's mercy is not limited to God's people.

> PSALM 145:8-9 (TLB)
> *Jehovah is kind and merciful, slow to get angry, full of love. He is good to everyone, and his compassion is intertwined with everything he does.*

According to Psalm 145:8-9, what are some of God's merciful qualities? _____

_____

_____

_____

_____

_____

_____

What do you think it means that God is "compassionate?"

_____

_____

_____

_____

_____

God indeed is compassionate. He knows our weaknesses and is "mindful that we are but dust." His tender heart is moved with love and kindness toward all His creatures. Therefore God reaches out in mercy to help and comfort those who are in distress.

PSALM 145:14-19 (TLB)
*The Lord lifts the fallen and those bent beneath their loads. The eyes of all mankind look up to you for help; you give them their food as they need it. You constantly satisfy the hunger and thirst of every living thing. The Lord is fair in everything he does, and full of kindness. He is close to all who call on him sincerely. He fulfills the desires of those who reverence and trust him; he hears their cries for help and rescues them.*

Psalm 145:14-19 describes many practical ways in which God demonstrates His mercy. List as many as you can find in the space below, putting them into your own words.

_____

_____

_____

_____

How does it make you feel to realize that the God of all power and holiness is also a compassionate, merciful God?

Explain your answer. _____

_____

_____

_____

It should bring us great comfort to know that the God of all creation is not cold and calloused. He cares intimately about even the smallest details of our lives and longs to reach out and touch us with His comfort.

It should not surprise us to realize that God's mercy goes far beyond man's mercy. The following project will help us see that.

## THE "GOD IS MERCIFUL TO ALL" PROJECT:

Jesus Himself once commented that His Father is kind even to those who are evil and ungrateful. In the project below, list the ways in which God demonstrates mercy to all men, then describe how most people respond to His acts of kindness.

| GOD'S MERCY | MAN'S USUAL RESPONSE |
|---|---|
| *God gives the sun's light and warmth each day* | *Man takes it for granted and complains* |
| *God gives long life* | *Man thinks he did it by his goodness or good health* |
| | |
| | |
| | |
| | |
| | |
| | |
| | |
| | |
| | |
| | |

*Mercy is a spontaneous act of compassion which can neither be demanded or earned. It is God, in His tenderness, withholding judgment from men, both good and evil, grateful and ungrateful. When God reaches down and cleanses a person from sin and then gives him eternal life, He is demonstrating His grace.*

## 2. GOD IS GRACIOUS TO ALL HIS CREATURES, BECAUSE MAN IS UTTERLY HELPLESS TO SAVE HIMSELF.

Most people believe that if they simply try to be a good person, God will accept them. The Bible makes it clear, though, that man has as much chance of saving himself as does a drowning man in the middle of the ocean. None!

The apostle Paul, in his letter to the Ephesians, explained the terrible predicament man is in.

EPHESIANS 2:1-3 (TLB)
*Once you were under God's curse, doomed forever for your sins. You went along with the crowd and were just like all the others, full of sin, obeying Satan, the mighty prince of the power of the air, who is at work right now in the hearts of those who are against the Lord. All of us used to be just as they are, our lives expressing the evil within us, doing every wicked thing that our passions or our evil thoughts might lead us into. We started out bad, being born with evil natures, and were under God's anger just like everyone else.*

According to this passage, what was our spiritual condition?

_____

_____

Ephesians 2:1-3 gives us three sources for our evil behavior. What are they?

_____

_____

_____

According to this passage, would you say our evil deeds are our own fault or someone else's? Explain your answer.

_____

_____

_____

It may come as a shock to realize how doomed and helpless sin has made us before God. It may even frighten you to think that when we sin we are obeying Satan. However, we cannot escape responsibility for our sin by saying, "the devil made me do it." We are all guilty. But we can never begin to appreciate the grace of God until we see how utterly incapable we are of doing good and saving ourselves.

## 3. GOD'S GRACE IS A FREE AND UNDESERVED GIFT.

It is human nature to be suspicious of getting "something for nothing." We are often too proud to "accept charity." In America, we feel we gain forgiveness the old-fashioned way: We *earn* it!

The Bible tells us otherwise. In Ephesians, Paul gives us God's plan of salvation.

EPHESIANS 2:4-9 (NIV)
*But because of his great love for us, God, who is rich in mercy, made us alive with Christ even when we were dead in transgressions — it is by grace you have been saved. And God raised us up with Christ and seated us with him in the heavenly realms in Christ Jesus, in order that in the coming ages he might show the incomparable riches of his grace, expressed in his kindness to us in Christ Jesus. For it is by grace you have been saved, through faith — and this not from yourselves, it is the gift of God — not by works, so that no one can boast.*

According to Ephesians 2, how are we made "alive with Christ?"

_____

This scripture passage says that "it is by grace you have been saved, through faith." What do you think that means?

_____

_____

Many people think that their good works will save them. Ephesians 2 says that is not true. Why do you think it is impossible for a person's good deeds to get him into heaven?

_____

_____

_____

_____

That forgiveness comes only by trusting in God's grace is one of the most important truths in the Bible. God's forgiveness is a free and undeserved gift from God and is not prompted by anything we do.

> ROMANS 11:6 (TLB)
> And if it is by God's kindness [grace], then it is not by their being good enough. For in that case the free gift would no longer be free — it isn't free when it is earned.

As we look at our own helplessness to save ourselves and recall the terrible judgment that we have escaped, we can only stand in awe and gratitude for the mercy and grace of God.

Because of the great forgiving heart of God, our hearts should be filled with praise and thanksgiving to Him. But God desires more than our words and feelings; He wants our whole lives.

## 4. GOD'S MERCY AND GRACE MOTIVATE US TO GIVE OUR WHOLE LIFE TO HIM.

When we truly realize how compassionate and merciful God is, we find that we have a strong desire to respond with something that will please Him. The apostle Paul, in his letter to the Romans, tells us what is first and foremost on the heart of God.

> ROMANS 12:1 (NIV)
> Therefore, I urge you, brothers, in view of God's mercy, to offer your bodies as living sacrifices, holy and pleasing to God — this is your spiritual act of worship.

What did Paul urge us to do in Romans 12:1, because of God's mercy?

_____

_____

What do you think he meant when he told us to offer our "bodies as living sacrifices?"

_____

_____

_____

_____

_____

_____

_____

_____

A sacrifice is something that we give up. It is usually something that is precious to us, that costs us. There is nothing more precious to most of us than our bodies. Our body is us! And that is what God wants. Us! He may never ask us to die for Him, but He wants us to live for Him. Are you willing?

The following project will help you to give the major areas of your life over to God ... if you mean it. It is encouraging to know that you are placing your life in the hands of an all-powerful, all-wise, all-loving, merciful God.

## THE "LIVING SACRIFICE" PROJECT:

Listed below are the major areas of your life. In the space provided, write a short prayer giving each area over to God's control. Then pray each prayer sincerely to God.

**MY HEART** _Lord, I give you first place in my heart. I want to love you more_

_than anyone else. I — give you my heart. Teach me to love with_

_your deep love._ _____

**MY MIND** _____

**MY TONGUE** _____

**MY EYES** _____

**MY EARS** _____

**MY HANDS** _____

**MY FEET** _____

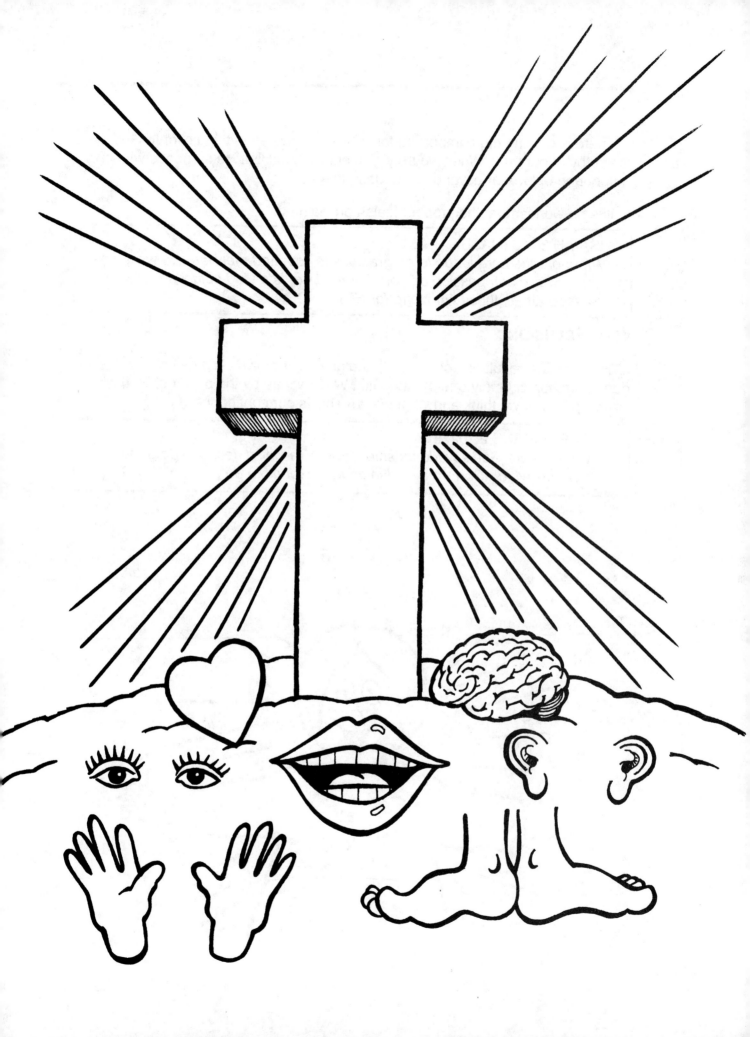

There is nothing more important for us than to give everything over to God. He is worthy of our trust. When we truly give our lives to Him, He responds with an outpouring of love far beyond our wildest dreams.

It is no wonder that the prophet Isaiah proclaimed:

ISAIAH 30:18 (NASB)
*Therefore the Lord longs to be gracious to you, and therefore He waits on high to have compassion on you. For the Lord is a God of justice; how blessed are all those who long for Him.*

## IN CONCLUSION

The practical result of God's mercy and grace in our lives is a daily demonstration of Godly energy and faith. What we are by the power of God will show up in how we think and what we do. This is our confidence:

EPHESIANS 2:10 (NIV)
*For we are God's workmanship, created in Christ Jesus to do good works, which God prepared in advance for us to do.*

# YOUR GOD MUST BE TRUSTWORTHY

# CHAPTER 9

During this series of studies, we have caught a glimpse of the power, knowledge, wisdom and sovereignity of God. Because of God's great power, it is easy to become overwhelmed with God's awesomeness and therefore want to withdraw from Him into insecurity and fear. Perhaps, in the back of your mind, you are troubled by the thought that God may become moody or unstable and wreak havoc on the world. If so, it is extremely comforting to know that God is totally reliable and trustworthy.

## WHAT IS THE TRUSTWORTHINESS OF GOD?

The trustworthiness of God declares that God can be counted on to be eternally unchanging and eternally true to His Word.

*THEREFORE, LET US EXAMINE WHY GOD, UNLIKE THE WORLD AROUND US, IS TRUSTWORTHY AND WHAT OUR RESPONSE SHOULD BE.*

## 1. GOD IS TRUSTWORTHY, BECAUSE HE IS ETERNAL.

It is mind-boggling to think about eternity. We quickly collapse from mental exhaustion when we try to think back through time to eternity past or forward to eternity future. But no matter which way we look into eternity, God has always and will always be there.

The Psalmist explains this staggering truth as follows:

> PSALM 90:1-2 (NIV)
> *Lord, you have been our dwelling place throughout all generations. Before the mountains were born, or you brought forth the earth and the world, from everlasting to everlasting you are God.*

What do you think Psalm 90:1-2 means when it says, "even from everlasting to everlasting, you are God?" _____

_____

_____

_____

_____

According to these verses, do you think the writer was frightened or comforted by realizing that God is eternal?

Explain your answer. _____

_____

_____

_____

_____

_____

The writer of Psalm 90 found great encouragement and strength from understanding that God has no beginning or end. Since God is eternal, He has never missed a thing that has happened in the universe! Nothing has escaped His notice. In addition, God has always been there and always will be there when we need Him.

But it is not enough to realize that God has always been and always will be. God, in fact, is not bound and limited by time like we are, as the apostle Peter declared:

> 2 PETER 3:8 (NASB)
> *But do not let this one fact escape your notice, beloved, that with the Lord one day is as a thousand years, and a thousand years as one day.*

What one fact did Peter want to make sure we did not miss?

_____

_____

_____

Whether one day or a thousand years goes by, it is all the same to God because He can see all of time, all the time. Knowing that God is not limited by time, how does that help you to trust Him?

_____

_____

_____

God is able to view our entire lives and all of history in an instant. Therefore, nothing catches Him off guard. He also understands how the smallest event or problem in our life fits into His eternal plan. He lives in eternity; He is not bound by the limitations of time.

Is it any wonder that God wants us to be excited that we know and love Him more than the temporal things of this life? In contrast to the fleeting moments of life on earth, eternity is linked to God. The writer of Psalms contrasted the eternal God with the temporal world when he wrote Psalm 102.

---

PSALM 102:25-27 (NIV)
*In the beginning you laid the foundations of the earth, and the heavens are the work of your hands. They will perish, but you remain; they will all wear out like a garment. Like clothing you will change them and they will be discarded. But you remain the same, and your years will never end.*

---

What does Psalm 102 say will happen to the universe around us?

_____

_____

By contrast, what does the writer of this psalm say will happen to God?

_____

_____

_____

The following project is designed to help you see how much wiser it is to trust an eternal God than people and temporal things.

## THE "WHO AND WHAT SHOULD I TRUST" PROJECT:

In the spaces below, list some of the people who impress you and compare the length of their lives with God.

| NAME OF PERSON IMPORTANT TO ME | NAME OF PERSON IMPORTANT TO ME | EXPECTED LIFE OF PERSON IMPORTANT TO ME |
| --- | --- | --- |
| _____ | _____ | _____ |
| _____ | _____ | _____ |
| _____ | _____ | _____ |
| _____ | _____ | _____ |
| _____ | _____ | _____ |

God is not subject to the same sufferings and afflictions that man is. Though man is weak, God is powerful. Though man is without understanding, God is wise. And all that God is now, He has always been and always will be, because He never changes.

## 2. GOD IS TRUSTWORTHY, BECAUSE HE NEVER CHANGES.

It is reassuring to know that God is forever the same. No one is more secure than God. He is not moved or changed by a fluctuating world. God never changes.

The God who rules the universe today is the same God who has ruled from eternity past and will rule to eternity future. God is not aging, maturing or evolving. He cannot get wiser, stronger or purer, because He is already perfect. God remains absolutely, eternally the same.

God Himself made that point clear through Malachi when He said:

> MALACHI 3:6 (NASB)
> *"For I, the Lord, do not change."*

In what ways do you think most people believe that God has changed over the

centuries? _____

_____

It is easy to think that because man has changed over the years, God has also. Many people identify God as cruel and wrathful in the Old Testament, but kind and merciful now. But God has not changed; only man's ideas of God have changed. God would as surely destroy the wicked cities of Sodom and Gomorrah today as He did 4,000 years ago!

It is important to remember that just because God is unchanging, He does not live in the past. God is not a doddering old man who speaks only ancient Hebrew. He has always possessed all knowledge. He knew everything about lasers, computers and robots ages before the ideas ever entered the mind of man!

The book of James reinforces this truth that God is incapable of change when it says:

> JAMES 1:17 (NIV)
> *Every good and perfect gift is from above, coming down from the Father of the heavenly lights, who does not change like shifting shadows.*

What do you think James meant when he wrote that God does not change "like

shifting shadows?" _____

_____

_____

God is as pure, intense and unchanging as if the sun were eternally at high noon. He never leaves us in doubt as to who He is or what He expects of us. He does not fill our lives with light one moment and deceptive darkness the next. How does knowing that God does not change

help you to trust Him? _____

_____

_____

God is not rattled by the constant changes, emergencies and crises that affect our lives. He is too powerful to be fearful, too wise to be confused and too sovereign to be frustrated. Because God is strong and stable, we should not be intimidated by the changing circumstances which surround us, as the writer of Psalm 46 declares:

> ### PSALM 46:1-3 (NASB)
> *God is our refuge and strength, a very present help in trouble. Therefore we will not fear, though the earth should change, and though the mountains slip into the heart of the sea; though its waters roar and foam, though the mountains quake at its swelling pride.*

According to Psalm 46, "God is our refuge and strength." Write down what you

think that means. _____

_____

_____

## THE "GOD IS OUR REFUGE" PROJECT:

The Bible says that God is a refuge where we can go when we are hurting. He is a fortress, strong and stable, where we can run when we are afraid. He is a rock of truth and our security in a crazy world. He is a shield to protect us from harm. And He is a stronghold to give us peace and rest when we're anxious and worried.

In the space below, write a short letter thanking God for His unchanging love, strength and protection.

_____

_____

_____

_____

_____

_____

_____

### 3. GOD IS TRUSTWORTHY, BECAUSE HE ALWAYS DOES WHAT HE SAYS.

Satan in the Garden of Eden deceived Eve into thinking that God was holding back on her. He created doubt as to God's love and persuaded her that God was not trustworthy. Adam and Eve failed to believe that God meant what He said, but they found out to their hurt (and ours) that they should have trusted God. Ever since that time God has been seeking those who would trust Him.

Noah, alone out of his whole generation, believed God when He said that the earth would be destroyed with a flood. For 120 years he built an ark in the face of scorn and rejection, but he was saved when the flood came. God did what He promised.

Abraham proved that God could be counted on, not one time but many. He moved to Canaan when God told him to. He learned through Isaac that God would do what He said. His life was spent finding out that when God spoke, it came true.

Job had so learned of God's trustworthiness that he could say in the midst of terrible suffering:

> JOB 13:15 (NKJV)
> *"Though He slay me, yet will I trust Him:"*

What does this tell you about Job and his confidence in God?

_____

_____

_____

_____

_____

_____

_____

_____

_____

Solomon, one of the wisest men that ever lived, advised his hearers with the following:

PROVERBS 3:5 (NIV):
*"Trust in the Lord with all your heart and lean not on your own understanding;*

Such counsel implies deep confidence in God. Why do you think God can be

trusted? Or why not? _____

_____

_____

The book of Hebrews speaks of what God wants when it talks of faith as trust.

HEBREWS 11:6 (NIV):
*And without faith it is impossible to please God, because anyone who comes to him must believe that he exists and that he rewards those who earnestly seek him.*

According to Hebrew 11:6, what is the most important thing you can _____

do for God? _____

_____

How do most of the people you know try to please God? _____

_____

Now put into your own words what you think faith means: _____

_____

_____

_____

## IN CONCLUSION

As we have seen, God is totally trustworthy. In a world that is passing away, God remains the Eternal One. In a world that is decaying, God remains forever the same.

God can be trusted with every aspect of our lives. He is the eternal, unchanging One who, unlike man, always keeps His word.

> NUMBERS 23:19 (NASB)
> *God is not a man, that He should lie, nor a son of man, that He should repent; has He said, and will He not do it? Or has He spoken, and will He not make it good?*

It is exciting to realize that we can know this God personally right now and for all eternity.

# YOUR GOD MUST BE A PERSON

In this discussion manual we have attempted to embark on the most incredible journey possible to the human soul. We have sought to travel to the heart of God to discover what He is really like. We have caught a glimpse of His awesome power and control over creation. We have gazed in reverence at His brilliant holiness and wisdom. We have been amazed at His tender mercy and grace. And we have been deeply moved by His love and compassion for sinners such as we!

An ever more astounding journey took place, however, nearly 2,000 years ago. God Himself personally took on human form and lived among us. Jesus Christ was a very real person in history, but He is also God's ultimate revelation of Himself to man. The writer of Hebrews said it best when he wrote:

> HEBREWS 1:1-3 (NASB)
> *God, after He spoke long ago to the fathers in the prophets in many portions and in many ways, in these last days has spoken to us in His Son, whom He appointed heir of all things, through whom also He made the world. And He is the radiance of His glory and the exact representation of His nature, and upholds all things by the word of His power.*

Although many people will acknowledge that Jesus was a great religious leader, many others deny or are ignorant of the fact that He is also God.

He is not merely a man who lived a perfect life. Neither is He simply the way to God. He is a living person whom we can know and love. He is God Himself! The apostle Paul confirms this fact in his letter to the Colossians:

COLOSSIANS 2:9 (TLB)
*For in Christ there is all of God in a human body.*

And in case you might reason that the idea of Jesus as God was fabricated by His disciples after His death, Jesus Himself made His views very clear. One day during His earthly ministry, a disciple named Philip asked Jesus to give the apostles a sneak peek at God the Father. This is how Jesus replied:

JOHN 14:9 (NIV)
*"Don't you know me, Philip, even after I have been among you such a long time? Anyone who has seen me has seen the Father."*

Were Jesus merely a man, He could never have defended such a claim. And yet He did claim to be God and His whole life was an exclamation point to that fact.

*THEREFORE LET US EXAMINE THE LIFE OF JESUS CHRIST TO SEE HOW HE REFLECTED PERFECTLY THE VERY NATURE OF GOD AND WHAT OUR RESPONSE SHOULD BE TO HIM.*

## 1. JESUS CHRIST IS ALL POWERFUL

We have seen in our study that God is all-powerful. If Jesus is God, we would expect Him to have all power too. Many people, however, only think of Jesus as the frail, helpless baby born in a manger on Christmas morning. But the Bible reveals that Jesus has awesome power, power that can only be attributed to God. In Colossians 1, the apostle Paul gives us the facts about Christ's power.

COLOSSIANS 1:15-17 (TLB)
*Christ is the exact likeness of the unseen God. He existed before God made anything at all, and, in fact, Christ himself is the Creator who made everything in heaven and earth, the things we can see and the things we can't; the spirit world with its kings and kingdoms, its rulers and authorities; all were made by Christ for his own use and glory. He was before all else began and it is his power that holds everything together.*

According to this passage, Jesus has incredible power. What does Colossians 1:15-17 say about Jesus' part in the creation of the universe? _____

_____

The apostle Paul writes that "it is his power that holds everything together." What do you think that means?

_____

_____

_____

It is amazing to consider that everything that has ever been created or ever will be created is there because of Jesus. Not only that, Christ is the One who, by His great power, holds the universe together! From the orbits of the mightiest planets to the orbits of the tiniest electrons, all things are held in place by Christ's powerful word.

While Jesus lived as a man on earth, He constantly demonstrated His great power. He healed the blind and lame instantly. He cast out demons with a word. He walked on water and calmed the stormy sea. He multiplied five loaves of bread and two small fish into enough food to feed 5,000 people!

But one day He astounded the people of Bethany by performing a miracle at the tomb of a man named Lazarus, who had been dead four days. John recorded what Jesus did.

> JOHN 11:43-45 (NIV)
> *When he said this, Jesus called in a loud voice, "Lazarus, come out!" The dead man came out, his hands and feet wrapped with strips of linen, and a cloth around his face. Jesus said to them, "Take off the grave clothes and let him go." Therefore many of the Jews who had come to visit Mary, and had seen what Jesus did, put their faith in him.*

What did Jesus do in John 11 to raise Lazarus from the dead?

_____

_____

Why do you think many of the Jews who witnessed this miracle put their faith in Jesus? _____

It must have been an incredible experience to stand at that tomb and watch a man who had been dead four days suddenly come alive. But what about Lazarus? Can you imagine what it must have been like for him?

As phenomenal as it was that Jesus could raise a man to life, it is even more fantastic to realize He had a part in raising *Himself* from the dead! The apostle John recorded Jesus' words very carefully.

> JOHN 10:17-18 (NASB)
> *"For this reason the Father loves Me, because I lay down My life that I may take it again. No one has taken it away from Me, but I lay it down on My own initiative. I have authority to lay it down, and I have authority to take it up again. This commandment I received from My Father."*

What authority did Jesus receive from His Father, according to this passage? _____

_____

_____

Jesus had the power to control all the details of His death, as well as bring Himself back to life again! How does this demonstrate that Jesus was God and not a mere man?

_____

_____

_____

Mere men have little control over the manner of their death. Death often comes without warning and against the individual will. Even in the tragedy of suicide, a person can take his life, but there is no one who has the power to bring himself back to life again. Jesus was unique. He showed the mighty power of God by raising Himself from the dead. The apostle Paul made a point of this when he wrote:

> ROMANS 1:4 (NIV)
> *Who through the Spirit of holiness was declared with power to be the Son of God by his resurrection from the dead: Jesus Christ our Lord.*

## 2. JESUS CHRIST IS HOLY.

We have seen in a previous study that God the Father is holy. He is high and exalted, separated from sinners and from sin itself. In fact, God detests sin with all His being and is eternally committed to stamping it out. And although Jesus lived and worked in a sinful world, He himself remained holy. The writer of Hebrews spoke of this aspect of Jesus' character when he wrote:

> HEBREWS 7:26 (TLB)
> *He is, therefore, exactly the kind of High Priest we need; for he is holy and blameless, unstained by sin, undefiled by sinners, and to him has been given the place of honor in heaven.*

Only God is truly holy. The writer of Hebrews explains what Christ's character is like. Look at Hebrews 7:26 and describe Him. _____

_____

_____

Could this description of Jesus be that of a mere man? Why or why not? _____

_____

Jesus was so confident of His absolute purity that He even challenged His enemies to find any fault in Him. Since they were unable to point to any sin He had committed, they chose other methods to discredit Him. They slandered His holy character and eventually sought His death in order to silence Him.

One of the incidents which demonstrated Jesus' hatred of sin, and which aroused the hatred of His enemies was His cleansing of the temple.

> JOHN 2:13-17 (NIV)
> *When it was almost time for the Jewish Passover, Jesus went up to Jerusalem. In the temple courts he found men selling cattle, sheep and doves, and others sitting at tables exchanging money. So he made a whip out of cords, and drove all from the temple area, both sheep and cattle; he scattered the coins of the money changers and overturned their tables. To those who sold doves he said, "Get these out of here! How dare you turn my Father's house into a market!" His disciples remembered that it is written: "Zeal for your house will consume me."*

According to John 2, what did Jesus do in the temple to vividly display His hatred

of sin? _____

_____

_____

Jesus felt deep and righteous anger toward those who had set up shop in the temple. Why do you think this was so repulsive to Jesus? _____

_____

_____

When Jesus cleansed the temple, He was demonstrating to the world that He was holy and that He had the power and authority to stamp out unholy and repulsive practices that dishonored God.

### 3. JESUS CHRIST IS LOVING.

We have seen in our study that God is love. All love comes from God and He is love itself. But for us to have a better grasp of God's love, Jesus came to earth as a love gift from the Father.

> JOHN 3:16 (NKJV)
> *For God so loved the world that He gave His only begotten Son, that whoever believes in Him should not perish but have everlasting life.*

John's record says that "God *so* loved the world." What do you think "so loved" means? _____

_____

_____

_____

According to this verse, "whoever believes in Him should not perish but have everlasting life." What do you think it means to "believe?" _____

_____

_____

To believe in Christ is much more than to simply agree in your mind that Jesus is God's Son. It is more than getting excited about who Jesus is. To believe is to commit your whole life to Him and to give Him the driver's seat.

Although Christ's love for us is shown in countless ways ever day, there is one event in history that proves beyond a shadow of a doubt that Jesus loves us. Paul wrote of that love in Ephesians.

> EPHESIANS 5:2 (TLB)
> *Be full of love for others, following the example of Christ who loved you and gave himself to God as a sacrifice to take away your sins. And God was pleased, for Christ's love for you was like sweet perfume to him.*

This passage shows Christ's love for us in a very tangible way. How did Christ prove that He loved us?

_____

_____

What do you think Ephesians 5:2 means when it says Christ was a "sacrifice to take away your sins?" _____

_____

_____

## IN CONCLUSION

Jesus Christ in His earthly life demonstrated the character of God — what God has revealed about Himself. As the greatest man this world has ever seen, Jesus of Nazareth displayed God's power, holiness and love. Jesus was and is God!

When Philip asked to see the Father, Jesus told him that he had already seen the Father. Jesus also said that He who did not honor the Son did not honor the Father who had sent Him. The ultimate answer to who God is will be found in Jesus Christ. He is God!

# MAKE UP YOUR MIND!

---

Throughout this discussion manual we have seen the characteristics which God reveals about Himself and have found them also in Jesus Christ. But there is a final step which must be faced.

*MAKE JESUS CHRIST **YOUR** GOD.*

Let's look together at what is involved and what our individual response to these truths should be.

## 1. JESUS CHRIST, GOD'S SON, DIED IN YOUR PLACE.

Jesus gave the ultimate proof of His love when He gave His life for us on the cross. He paid the full penalty for our sin by dying in our place. Because He was totally innocent of all sin, Jesus did not deserve to die. We do! But Christ willingly took the full brunt of God's anger against sin upon Himself. He died for our sins.

> 1 JOHN 4:10 (NIV):
> *This is love: not that we loved God, but that he loved us and sent his Son as an atoning sacrifice for our sins.*

From this statement, what proof do you have that God loves you? _____

_____

The apostle Peter emphasized this important truth when he wrote:

> 1 PETER 2:24 (NIV):
> *He himself bore our sins in his body on the tree, so that we might die to sins and live for righteousness; by his wounds you have been healed.*

For whom did Christ die and what was the purpose of His death? _____

_____

_____

## 2. JESUS CHRIST, GOD'S SON, OFFERS HIS LIFE TO YOU.

Although Christ died for the sins of everyone who has ever lived or will ever live, forgiveness is not automatic. Some people will experience God's forgiveness and receive eternal life. Others will not. The apostle John spoke about what determines where a person will spend eternity in 1 John 5:1-13:

> 1 JOHN 5:11-13 (NIV):
> *And this is the testimony: God has given us eternal life, and this life is in his Son. He who has the Son has life; he who does not have the Son of God does not have life. I write these things to you who believe in the name of the Son of God so that you may know that you have eternal life.*

The apostle John speaks of two basic categories of people in the world. According to 1 John 5:11-13, what are they?

_____

_____

What do you think it means when John says, "He who has the Son has life?" _____

_____

_____

The Bible tells us that every person who has recognized his sin, has turned away from it and has placed his faith in Jesus alone to save him, receives eternal life. Are you certain that you have done this? If you are not sure, listen to God's voice today and open your heart to Jesus, His Son.

## 3. JESUS CHRIST, GOD'S SON, WAITS FOR YOU TO RECEIVE HIM.

The last book of the Bible, in talking about Jesus Christ, presents Him as follows:

> REVELATION 3:20 (NIV):
> *"Here I am! I stand at the door and knock. If anyone hears my voice and opens the door, I will come in and eat with him, and he with me."*

When God has finished all He wants to do and has said all He wants to say, it comes down to this very personal matter of what *you* do with Jesus Christ.

## A PRAYER TO MAKE JESUS YOUR GOD.

We receive God's love and forgiveness by receiving Christ into our lives and trusting in Him alone to take away our sin. Sincere, heart-felt prayer is a good way for us to express our faith. If you are being honest with God, and you really want Christ to come in and take charge of your life, He will. The following prayer may be helpful to you.

**LORD JESUS, I SEE THAT I HAVE FAILED YOUR HOLY REQUIREMENTS AND DESERVE ONLY YOUR WRATH. BUT I THANK YOU THAT YOU LOVE ME AND DIED TO PAY THE FULL PENALTY FOR MY SIN. RIGHT NOW, I ASK YOU TO COME INTO MY LIFE AND SAVE ME. I TURN AWAY FROM MY SIN AND INVITE YOU TO TAKE YOUR RIGHTFUL PLACE AS MY LORD AND SAVIOR. THANK YOU FOR GIVING ME YOUR ETERNAL LIFE.**

## IN CONCLUSION

The result of our discussion and study in this manual is that we now see that the awesome God is personally knowable. In fact, this God wants us to commune with Him and enjoy His fellowship. He has made it possible for us to be right in His sight, because of what His Son, Jesus Christ has done. We can know God only by receiving Jesus Christ into our lives. When we do, He as God does what He has promised, makes Himself real to us and lives in us to guarantee that we will live with God forever.

# NOTES

_____

_____

_____

_____

_____

_____

_____

_____

_____

_____

_____

_____

_____

_____

_____

_____

# NOTES

# ABOUT SHEPHERD MINISTRIES

Shepherd Ministries is an organization meeting the needs of youth and serving as a resource to church youth groups through several different areas:

- **Publications** — With the writing skill of Dawson McAllister and others, Shepherd offers youth resource manuals for spiritual growth and maturity. Currently fifteen books are published to assist youth in their relationships with God, parents, and others. Leaders' guides are available for many of these topics. Beyond the written page, Shepherd produces videos which touch the the pulse of the American student. Whether the topic concerns one's self-esteem, how to get along with parents, or any other of the thirteen topics, the videos capture the attention of the student culture. The latest product, "Life 101: Learning To Say 'YES' to Life!" is a two-part video designed for the public school. Part one was purposely made for general assemblies and describes the problem of teenage suicide. Part two, to be shown outside of class time, gives the ultimate answer in Jesus Christ. For a list of publications offered by Shepherd, locate the order form found in the back of this book.

- **Student Conferences** — The backbone of Shepherd is the weekend conferences held in the larger cities of the nation. With the ministry of music and praise from Todd Proctor, Al Holley and others, and the teaching of Dawson McAllister, students eagerly attend these memorable events. This past year over 82,000 students attended these weekend events.

- **Youth Minister Conference** — A weeklong conference presently held during the fall in Dallas, this event is designed to minister to the youth pastor or worker and spouse. "Youth Ministry" is a joint venture of Shepherd Ministries and Rapha, and seeks to encourage, challenge, and assist youth ministers and their spouses.

- **Parent Seminar** — "Preparing Your Teenager for Sexuality" video seminar. Available to churches as a one-day event, Dawson teaches this seminar via giant screen video. Aaron Shook, a Christian singer/songwriter, leads the seminar and provides live music. This seminar equips parents with a step-by-step method for teaching kids God's view of sex. "Preparing Your Teenager for Sexuality" is also available as a stand-alone video series.

- **Television** — Dawson McAllister's mission is to reach the American student. Though many will not darken the door of a church, all of them will turn the dial of a television. A series of three prime-time tv specials were produced and aired in 22 of the largest cities in America to reach those students. In Dallas in 1989 the program, "Too Young To Die" took first place in the Neilsen ratings for that evening hour.

- **Radio** — The newest tool to reach the American teenager is live call-in radio entitled, "Dawson McAllister Live." This one-hour weekly satellite program brings troubled, confused teenagers into contact with straight talk and clear Biblical guidance. Each student who calls and receives Dawson's compassionate counsel on the air represents thousands of others with similar problems. Not only do they hear Dawson's advice, but the students are invited to call for one-on-one counseling on a toll-free line.

# Shepherd Ministries
## ...from Dawson McAllister

## ORDER FORM

### MANUALS

| MANUALS | STUDENT Price | Code | Qty | TEACHER Price | Code | Qty | TRANSPARENCIES Price | Code | Qty |
|---|---|---|---|---|---|---|---|---|---|
| Student Relationships Volume I | 8.75 | 2010 | | 6.95 | 2011 | | 43.95 | 2080 | |
| Student Relationships Volume II | 8.75 | 2012 | | 6.95 | 2013 | | 43.95 | 2081 | |
| Student Relationships Volume III | 8.75 | 2014 | | 6.95 | 2015 | | 43.95 | 2082 | |
| A Walk With Christ to the Cross | 8.95 | 2030 | | 5.95 | 2031 | | 24.95 | 2085 | |
| Through the Resurrection | 8.95 | 2032 | | | | | | | |
| Student Discipleship Volume I | 8.50 | 2020 | | | | | | | |
| Student Discipleship Volume II | 8.50 | 2022 | | | | | | | |
| Who are you, Jesus? | 7.95 | 2040 | | 5.95 | 2041 | | | | |
| Who are you, God? | 7.95 | 2050 | | 5.95 | 2051 | | | | |
| You, God, and Your Sexuality | 3.95 | 2060 | | | | | | | |
| Preparing Your Teenager for Sexuality (For Parents) | 6.95 | 2065 | | | | | | | |
| Handbook of Financial Faithfulness | 6.95 | 8010 | | | | | | | |
| Dawson Speaks Out on Self Esteem & Loneliness | 3.95 | 2070 | | | | | | | |
| Search for Significance | 7.95 | 2075 | | 10.00 | 2076 | | | | |
| The Great War | 7.95 | 2090 | | | | | | | |
| Brand Name Christians | 6.95 | 2045 | | | | | | | |

Mail completed order blank to:
**SHEPHERD MINISTRIES**
2845 W. Airport Frwy. Suite 137
Irving, TX 75062
(214) 570-7599

### VIDEOS

| VIDEOS | PURCHASE Price | Code | Qty |
|---|---|---|---|
| A Walk with Christ to the Cross | 189.95 | 4120 | |
| When Tragedy Strikes | 79.95 | 4740 | |
| Dawson Speaks Out on Self Esteem and Loneliness | 169.95 | 4050 | |
| Christianity in Overalls (4 Part) | 169.95 | 4020 | |
| Straight Talk About Friends and Peer Pressure (5 Part) | 169.95 | 4040 | |
| Student Workbooks (Set of 5) | 6.25 | 4340 | |
| Preparing Your Teenager for Sexuality | 189.95 | 4100 | |

### VIDEOS

| VIDEOS | PURCHASE Price | Code | Qty |
|---|---|---|---|
| How to Get Along With Your Parents (4 Sessions) | 149.95 | 4031 | |
| Student Workbooks (Set of 5) | 9.75 | 4330 | |
| Papa, Please Love Me! | 169.95 | 4060 | |
| Tough Questions About Sex | 59.95 | 4010 | |
| Too Young to Die | 69.95 | 4750 | |
| Making Peace with Dad | 69.95 | 4730 | |
| Kids in Crisis | 69.95 | 4720 | |
| Life 101 | 99.95 | 4800 | |
| How to Know You're in Love | 29.99 | 4760 | |

### SHIP TO:

Name _____

Organization _____

Position _____

Address _____

City _____ State _____ Zip _____

Phone ( ) _____

Total Order _____

Shipping _____

Total Due _____

☐ Please bill me
☐ Payment enclosed

For postage & handling: Add 8% of the total amt.; minimum charge - $2.00. For orders over $150.00, please add 5% of the total amt. For special RUSH shipments (2-day UPS or First Class), add 13% of the total; minimum charge — $4.00.